ERNEST HOLMES

SEMINAR LECTURES

(REVISED)

ERNEST HOLMES

SEMINAR LECTURES

(REVISED)

Georgia C. Maxwell

Editor

SCIENCE OF MIND COMMUNICATIONS
Los Angeles, California

Science of Mind Communications Edition - January 1987
Second Printing - May 1992
Copyright © 1955 by Georgia C. Maxwell

Published by SCIENCE OF MIND COMMUNICATIONS
3251 W. Sixth Street - P.O. Box 75127
Los Angeles, California 90075
Originally published by
Willing Publishing Company
San Gabriel, California

Printed in the United States of America
ISBN 0-911336-83-4

Cover design: Robert Allen

DEDICATION

This book, in keeping with the desires of Dr. Holmes and of the editor, is dedicated to the League of Religious Science Practitioners in recognition of its successful prayer work on behalf of many, many students and clients, and in acknowledgement of its devoted allegiance to the United Church of Religious Science, its affiliated churches, and many activities.

Georgia C. Maxwell

CONTENTS

PREFACE

The material in this book was originally given as a series of lectures by Dr. Ernest Holmes before leaders, practitioners and members of the Church of Religious Science, high up in the Sierra Nevada mountains of California, at its first summer conference in 1953. We believe that the message of peace and love which they contain is one that millions of people in this hectic age will want to read and study. Hence this book.

I express grateful acknowledgment to Dr. Willis Kinnear, Editor Emeritus of *Science of Mind* Magazine, for his wise counsel and aid, which were extended throughout the preparation of the manuscript.

Georgia C. Maxwell

NOTE TO THE REVISED EDITION

The original edition of this book, published in 1955, contained numerous typographical errors and inconsistencies, as well as minor instances of unclear style. Those problems have been corrected in this edition. In addition, the Dedication, Preface, and some chapter titles have been updated. The guiding purpose behind all revisions has been to clarify the ideas of Dr. Holmes, and all changes were made with the advice and agreement of the book's original editor, Georgia C. Maxwell.

FOREWORD

Dr. Ernest Holmes

Generally speaking, we think of such a gathering as this as a "retreat." But in Religious Science a spiritual retreat really is a "spiritual advance." We should acquire a greater consciousness in uniting our thought with each other in a common cause and purpose for which we work, and upon which our whole practice is based: *a consciousness of the Presence of God within everything and everyone.* Our spiritual advance, then, is devoted to a deeper awareness, a higher perception, and a greater realization of spiritual Truth, the reality of a Divine Presence, whose impulsion is love, and a Universal Principle which acts as law.

As we are gathered together here this week in quietness and peace, let us keep our thoughts turned to the Divine Presence within us and within each other. Let us bless ourselves and each other, that what we do shall blossom into the fruit of the Spirit. Deeply desiring that we become more aware of the love we have for each other and the world, may our consciousness be opened to the mission of the Father's service and to a deeper understanding of Life.

As this great mountain range, with the sun rising in glory over its peaks, keeps watch over the valleys, so may our vision rise from the mountain tops of an exalted spiritual feeling and keep watch over the valleys of our experience, that they may be refreshed by the perennial rain from Heaven and be sheltered, protected and productive.

Here in the beauty of nature, in all its grandeur, may we open our consciousness to the Divine influx and make of ourselves a fit organ and instrument of the Infinite. May there come to each of us an inward deep peace, as the trees whisper to us, and the strength of these rugged hills—snow-capped, sun-kissed, founded on the eternal rock of everlasting Truth —talk to us.

Infinite spirit within and around us, such gifts as we have we give to Thee. Amen.

ERNEST HOLMES

SEMINAR LECTURES
(REVISED)

Let us turn our attention to that Divine Presence within, which is both the center and circumference of our real being. It is the Infinite Presence which inhabits eternity and finds a dwelling place in our own consciousness. We recognize It as the only authority there is. We know we are one with It and in It, for there is no separation from It. Our own consciousness is the very depth and height of Its Being and is one with all that It is. And so let it be.

*E.H. ** *

Note: The meditations which open each chapter were written either by Ernest Holmes (E.H.) or by Georgia Maxwell (G.M.). Authorship is indicated in each case by the appropriate initials.

CHAPTER ONE

The Science of Prayer

The perception of wholeness is the consciousness of healing! Let us have this clear—we have no dogmatic belief! My opinion is not necessarily yours, yours need not necessarily be mine. However, there do seem to be certain fundamental ideas, which have been discovered in the metaphysical field during the time of its existence and which experience has verified. There are certain philosophic truths and spiritual intuitions that the ages have contributed to the sum total of our knowledge, just as there are certain scientific facts, which, because they can be demonstrated and reproduced at will, determine basic principles. These ideas and truths we share in common.

Religious Science is based on the concept that the Universe is one system and only one, not two; that it is ruled by law and impelled by love; that there is a self-existent Cause which didn't make Itself. God didn't make it, we didn't make it, it wasn't made. The Truth is that which *is*. It is inconceivable to think of a time when God began to be God, or Law began to be Law. We neither create God nor Law.

There is, in my estimation, no God that thought of Himself or Itself as beginning, or as creating Law, because in eternalities there is neither a beginning nor an end. We do believe that there is an infinite self-knowingness, which we call

15

the Spirit, "Our Father which art in Heaven," God, the first Cause, or This Thing Called Life. We believe that this is personal, warm, colorful, and responsive to that which communes with It, and that each of us is an individualized center in It, without being an individual separate from It. There is only *One* of whatever "It" is. We are rooted in the One, which is an Infinite Unity objectively producing limitless variety. Therefore, God is uniquely individual and uniquely personal to each one of us. In other words, we are uniquely individual to God, and God is uniquely personal to each one of us. This is not a contradiction of logic or of mathematics. It is an affirmation that all numbers start with the original digit of one, and if you or I perceive that original one and its variations, we perceive it only because it has a relationship to us, which must respond at the level of our perception of it.

We did not put the mountains here. We perceive them because there is, as Emerson said, "One Mind common to all individual men," or as Kant said, "there is awakened in us an intuition in a common field." Berkeley stated "there cannot be a perception without a perceiver." Since there are many things which I do not perceive there must be a perceiver to which, in which, and of which, all things exist. We do progressively see more but we believe that there is that within us which is the perceiver, the original perceiver now uniquely individualized within Itself as each one of us. Each of us is a center in the consciousness of God. Therefore, we believe Spirit. I believe we are not one in God or one with God, but we are one *of* God. Although the identity is the same in essence, it is not the same in degree. If there were a sameness in degree, we would have already exhausted the possibility of the Infinite and having done so our continual existence would be a cosmic tragedy, because there would be no place to go and nothing to see. Everything would have been used up.

We believe that as there is only One Spirit, there is only One Creative Medium, a neutral, impersonal Law existing everywhere. You may also call it the Soul of the Universe. It is not opposed to but complementary to the Spirit. The Spirit is the Father and the Soul is the Mother. The Greeks taught the idea of the pneuma, the Spirit, and the psyche, the Soul or the womb of the universe. Some schools of thought call it universal subjectivity. It is, we might say, a universal subjectivity which is subconscious but not unconscious. I am not referring to the subconscious or unconscious of psychology.

We do not believe that there is any such thing as your individual subconscious or subjective mind. We do believe, however, that each one of us has an atmosphere in this universal field, which, because of the action of Law, makes it appear as though we have an individual mind, but we haven't. We believe everything that psychology teaches us that we can prove to be true but we correlate that knowledge with a greater concept.

Religious Science does not teach that there is an individual psyche or an individual soul, or even that there is an individual body. It does teach that out of a vast universality the Spirit is *individualized* as Spirit, as Soul, as Body, in a unique way as each one of us, which is proven by the fact that no two thumb prints are alike. There is no question about the logic of this. It keeps faith with the great spiritual intuitions of the ages, and I have no doubt whatsoever that it is true.

In our discussions of the fundamentals of Spiritual Mind healing and demonstration, let us keep in mind the difference between the psychological concept and the metaphysical concept of the psyche. We can do this without disturbing the psychological concept, for we understand what it means. For instance, a baby is born and as it grows into adolescence and adulthood it gains awareness and an understanding of spiritual values, and so the psychologist conceives that the child is born out of something which is perfect within the baby. It is said that the baby's only fear is of loud noises and falling. It has to learn to be afraid. It has yet to learn all about "hell." That comes when it grows old enough, intellectually and emotionally, to accept and believe and feel what the world deems is necessary for it to believe. We go through this world pretty much hypnotized from the cradle to the grave. The psychological concept is that the baby is born out of feeling, or the original "Id," or an impulsion toward self-expression. Troward called this "the true unconscious." The Id simply means the "It."

The first law of that feeling, or the first law of the emotional life, is that the libido must have an object. Love must love something. The singer must sing, the dancer must dance, the prayer must pray, the farmer must plow, the intelligent Spirit-Life must express life—the libido *must* have an object. Why? Because the object *is* the self-expression or the manifestation of the Infinite. In other words, the dynamic power of the Id of Freud is the insistent cosmic urge of our own conviction. Jesus said, "The wind bloweth where it listeth and no man knoweth from whence it cometh or where it goeth, and so is every one who is born of the Spirit." This is a mystical saying. Again he said, "And no man has ascended up into Heaven except he who came down from Heaven, even the son of man who is in Heaven." Analyzing this statement, we find he is saying that Heaven *is*, but no man is ever going to go up there unless he came down from there, and nobody can either go up or down unless he is already there! The trip is in his imagination only.

18

The libido must have an object. If there isn't one, the impulsion of the individual creative urge plus the dynamics of the universal nature of this urge turns on its nature and goes back to the self. This is the meaning of all repression and all complex. Here is an example. Did you ever get enthusiastic about something and rush up to someone and say, "I have the greatest idea!" Then he deflatingly says, "Yeah?" Then you wish you were dead? That's frustration! The libido didn't find an object and so its energy turns within to depress. You see, life is made to fulfill itself. The ancients said "God is pure desire." I think that is a very good definition. The libido must have an object and lacking one it returns to itself, carrying the creative energy of its own impulsion back into what Kunkel called "an unlived state." This is a very good expression, denoting the unlived lives within us.

The next law of our being is that the ego must not be rejected. We must feel wanted, needed and loved. All feeling of aggression is merely the attempt to cover up inner repression. All superiority complexes are inferiority complexes working aggressively to escape the hurt wound of the heart. The ego must not be rejected. It has to be wanted, needed and loved.

It may seem unnecessary to discuss these psychological actions and reactions but they must be explained for we must know that what we do in our work isn't isolated, but that it is completely common-sensible. For instance, we believe in what Emerson called "the law of parallels." He said in his essay on the laws of thought that he waited the advent of any person who could liken all the laws of thought to laws of nature, and that when that happened God Himself would give praise. Why? Because someone would have found the key, we will say, to the kingdom of God. Now this is in accord with the Hermetic teachings—as above, so beneath; as below, so above; what is true on one plane is true on all. I believe that if I were a physicist, I could prove everything I believe metaphysically through the science of physics. If I were an electrician and understood electronics, I could prove it through that science. Einstein has proved it mathematically. The universe is one system—as above, so beneath; as below, so above; what is true on one plane is true on all. Therefore, I believe that for every law in physics there is a corresponding law of mind; for every law of attraction, of polarity, of chemical affinity or repulsion there is a law of mind, and it is not another law but the same one.

The universe is one system and it is not a system where there is a vast spiritual system "up there" and a great mental one "right here" and then another physical system "down below." The physical is the mental, the mental is the spiritual, the spiritual is the mental and the physical and it is all one universe. The mental and physical aspects are merely the modes of self-expression and it is *all* right where we are.

So what does the analyst, counselor, psychiatrist or psychoanalyst do? He goes back through the life history of the individual to his birth, brings the infant up to the experience of adulthood and leaves him still as a child, but childlike, not childish. If the analyst accomplishes his purpose, the individual is brought to self-awareness. I am not going to discuss all the processes by which it is done, for that would take hours of time. The techniques are merely incidental to getting a result, and what shall that be? It will be that the nature which was there at birth shall be present now in the same way it was at birth, having merely preserved the experiences of life but having eliminated the curse of them. This is all the analyst can ever do. This is all doctors can do. They merely aid nature.

20

We believe in medicine, surgery, psychiatry and psychology; we believe in anything and everything that aids. Our system of thinking excludes nothing; it is all-inclusive.

I am not making an assumption, as Whitman did when he said, "I doubt not that there are other eyes behind these eyes," or as Browning, who said, "Our purpose is not to create but to loose this imprisoned splendour." Swedenborg taught the law of correspondence and Emerson taught the law of parallels. Were they not making an assumption, perhaps without even knowing it, such as the Platonists did when they said everything here is a copy of a pattern "over yonder"? The Platonists were the finest intellectual thinkers the world has ever known. That is why it has been stated that seventy-five percent of the Christian philosophy came from the Greeks and twenty-five percent from the Jewish tradition. They assumed that everything in the visible world has a pattern in the invisible, which they called "over yonder," and by this they meant that which is identical with Jesus' concept that "The Kingdom of God is within you; be ye, therefore, perfect, even as your Father which is in Heaven is perfect."

Plotinus said that whenever any organ of our body seems to lose its connection with its pattern "over yonder" and is in pain, its whole longing is to get back to its pattern that it may be made whole. Jesus said to seek first this pattern of the kingdom which is within all things. Every one of these schools taught what the ancient intuition perceived and now modern science is proving it; psychosomatic medicine is proving it in every way.

There is a perfect pattern and we believe in it, and the perfect pattern is where we are and not somewhere else. It is already within us; this is the divine incarnation—the involution. You and I had nothing to do with it, in my estimation, and I hope you will understand when I say that I think God

21

had nothing to do with it. If I said God created the pattern, I would be saying God created God, and if God created God, what created the thing that made it possible for God to create God? It is known in all logic, and reason, and common sense, that when you arrive at an ultimate you must accept its nature.

It is the nature of Reality that it consists of infinite compulsion, infinite intelligence, infinite love, infinite self-giving-ness. It must create, having limitless desire to project Itself, and come into the fruition of experiencing Itself. It has no frustration and no inhibition. Nor could It do anything contrary to Its nature, and it is the nature of the Infinite Reality that it shall be this pattern about which we are speaking. That is why I say I do not think God made the pattern because the pattern is God *as* that aspect.

Thinking straight or straight thinking is a tough proposition. It calls for impersonalizing your thought and not being afraid of where it takes you, and above everything else, the ability to lay your own opinions out on the table and analyze them and get free from the burden of the thought that they are yours and you would like them to be true. This is one of the most difficult propositions we have, for *Truth is not what we believe!* We shall be fortunate when we believe the Truth, for in believing it we may come to understand it.

The divine pattern is the pattern of God and I had nothing to do with it and I can't change it. There it is. If I break a leg and can get back to the spiritual reality of my being, I shall be made whole, not because the spiritual reality is pleased with me or that there is a power which will do it for me. Rather, it is because the pattern *is* perfect and when we stand in its light, that which was imperfect disappears. Therefore, what we have to do is to produce a disappearing act in treatment, literally, or as Emerson said, ''get our bloated nothingness

22

out of the way." This is all that psychology or medicine can do. One says, let us treat the physical instrument for circulation, assimilation and elimination so that there is no stagnation, infection and death. The other says let us treat the psyche so that the original craving for self-expression shall come to the surface without interception or repression. Now this is what we do without denying the patching up of the body. If I break a leg, I will go and get it patched up.

In psychology it is said that sublimation is the deflection of the energy of the libido into other avenues and purposes. In other words, it isn't enough to say the conflict doesn't exist. The actual energy that creates has to be transmuted into another action so that the release of tension in the impulsion for self-expression shall dissipate into an act which is creative. That is why it is that, if you are creative, you are never happy until you create. You actually put yourself into the object of your adoration. Because of this we can see that it is the most difficult thing in the world to get rid of superstition and it is the hardest thing in the world to think straight. It is very hard to get rid of our devils, because unless the energy is transmuted or sublimated into something different, there will be a new devil of frustration.

In the "Vision of Sir Launfal," the knight travels all the world over in search of the Holy Grail, and as an old man he comes back to the roadside where he started his journey and there finds a beggar. In the beggar he discovers that which he had not found in his search.

> In search of Him but to thyself repair; wait thou within the silence dim and thou shalt find him there . . . at last I behold in thee an image of Him who died on the tree.

It was the first time he ever knew what "Christ" meant; the first time he ever drank from the Chalice of God. It was the first time that he understood that the cross itself is but a symbol of unity. It was the first time his idea of evil was actually sublimated or transmuted into another kind of essence, another kind of Mecca.

The perception of wholeness and the consciousness of healing is the "I Am," but it doesn't appear to be that way. We must have, first of all, an intellectual and emotional conviction, unless we are going to approach it by intercession or superstition, both of which should be eliminated forever from our way of thinking. Do not revert to the old superstitions—don't do it in the name of common sense! You are redeemed from them. Every day say to yourself that the mind shall be unstopped and the Spirit unleashed!

That which the intellect refuses to accept cannot become a part of our conscious action; that which the heart will not listen to cannot become part of our unconscious motivation. God speaks to the heart but what is in the heart must be translated through the intellect or you will have feeling without form. "Words without thoughts cannot to Heaven go." Techniques create a mold only, which must be filled with the consciousness of the feeling and which makes everything come alive and is called "the spirit of the letter of the law." There must be feeling *and* the mold.

We must have a belief that isn't borrowed but is something born in ourselves. There is a perfect pattern; there is a spiritual body. My body is that spiritual body. The ancients said the illusion of mind and the illusion of matter, called Maya, was two-fold, and they said you have to penetrate the one and then the other in order to heal. They understood the psychic field of confusion and "many tongues." Paul said it was better to speak ten words with understanding than ten thousand words in confusion and ignorance. We have to believe both intellectually and through our feeling and the two must come together. One is the letter and the other is the spirit, and I believe that we have to believe, with feeling, without going into an emotional fit. I do not deny the feeling because I couldn't live without it, but the feeling must take form.

In practice, then, we have to create a big feeling of wholeness, and the one who has the greatest feeling of wholeness and the greatest subjective embodiment of this wholeness will speak from the greatest degree of wholeness. When it comes to the actual use of technique he knows that there is no such thing as an individual spirit, an individual mind, or an individual body. As yet most people are not ready to accept this, but time will demonstrate that the inspiration and the spiritual theory of the illumination of the ages has never yet told the world one single lie!

We want to embody the one Spirit, one Mind, and one Body; we are all using It. For instance, it is said that there is only one pattern for all human eyes. Why is this? It demonstrates the universality of an idea and if you see it everywhere, there is revealed the individualization of it, but the individualization is always tied back to its universality. The perception of universality inevitably leads to the perception of individuality or individualization, and the perception of individualization inevitably leads to the perception of universality. It is the play of the one upon the other that produces Cosmic unity, that enables God to see Himself in us, as He is in Himself. We couldn't exist unless this were true, for this is what we are. The perception of the only perceiver is not the act of perceiving that which isn't and endeavoring to make it true, but individualizing that which is inherent in the constitution of the perceiver, ad infinitum!

The best spiritual mind practitioner will be the one who

combines the definite knowledge of his technique, where it is necessary, with the consciousness of wholeness. However, everything isn't whole that claims to be whole. This is where we miss the mark. For instance, let us take the thought of love, kindness and compassion. We cannot speak what we do not know. Remember, we are speaking the feeling—something that is alive—into a form that the intellect has consciously created, just as you would make a box with wood, hammer, saw and nails. This is the mechanical, technical act; this is making the mold, but the mold will not do anything until something is put into it, which is the spirit, the conviction, the feeling. Now if the universe is love, and we hate, our hate inhibits the action of love to us. This is what I mean when I say the perception of wholeness is the consciousness of healing, and it is! We must have a perception of love, of compassion, and of givingness. We may say we have it, or we say we will do everything for it, but do we have it?

We can apply this truth in a thousand ways. Someone will come to us for help who hasn't the consciousness of love. His ego has been rejected and his libido has not found an object. This is, by the way, what is back of a majority of all diseases. It sounds simple enough, but have we love enough to cover every sense of fear,—hate, being cast out, not being wanted or needed or loved? There is enough love to cover it, but do we have enough to uncover his? He has it but we have to uncover it. If *we* do not have it, we won't heal him.

We are not acquainted with wholeness while we would hurt or dislike anything that lives. We are acquainted with some wholeness. We have some love and if we have more love than another individual has hate, we can heal the hate with the love because the one will cover the other, for that is the way love works. We must come to the place where love shall automatically heal all the wounds! I love a few people and you love a few people. That is probably the greatest joy in life, for there is nothing else that equals love and friendship. Nothing else in the world compensates for it. "It is not to be bought or sold at sea, it's the treasure of Heaven, it's the lodestone of Heaven and it's the gift of Life, and it's all there is that is worthwhile."

Now suppose there are six people of whom I am very fond; these six I love very much. Suppose, theoretically, I could love everyone I meet as much as I love those six. Would I love those six less? No, of course not. It is very difficult to let go of the little, and we cannot take hold of the big unless we let go of the little. Why are we afraid to do this? It is because we do not know how terrific love is; we don't know what it means. We don't know how to feel in its presence!

Can we even now, psychologically or in any way other than by some divine interior intuition or self-awareness, know what it would mean to have the thrill of love pass through our being each time we met a person as we walked down the street? Such an ecstasy would make such a terrific impact on our soul that we couldn't stand it! It would shatter us.

We will never be good teachers of the Science of Mind until we understand how to give a scientific treatment even if we have to go through a drill process until we know it. Have we enough love, however, to cover the hate in the student? When someone comes to us with fear, whatever *we* are afraid of will block the clearance for him because he is sitting in our lap. He is clasping us to his breast. Have we generated so much faith that there is nothing to cause us to fear? When someone told Emerson that the world was going to end the next day, he said, "That's all right with me. I can get along without it; I've gotten along without it for a long time." And he said,

The lords of life, the lords of life,—
Little man, least of all,
Among the legs of his guardians tall,
Walked about with puzzled look.
Him by the hand dear Nature took,
Dearest Nature, strong and kind,
Whispered, 'Darling, never mind!
Tomorrow they will wear another face,
The founder thou; these are thy race'!

Are we big enough, is our faith so great, that someone sitting in a shadow shall find that the sun is in its zenith and casts no shadow? It will cast a shadow commensurate with any fear that we, ourselves, have. This is why all of our healing is self-healing. There is only One Mind! Is our joy in life uncontaminated by psychic depressions and morbid religious ideas of sin and salvation, both of which are the two ends of one psychological morbidity? Do we have enough joy in life so that no sadness or depression can interfere? If we have, someone who is sad and sitting beside us will begin to feel that joy. We can treat impersonally, use all the qualities of thought, the emotions of our hearts, the feelings of our minds, and the aspirations of our souls but is there peace enough in us so that those who come to us will not cast a shadow of confusion? Jesus said that if the blind lead the blind, they will both fall into the ditch. There must be a seeing eye.

It is said in modern psychology that during an analysis, if the analyst gets back to the place of conflict in the consciousness of the one being analyzed, where perhaps the patient began to hate his father, and has a corresponding feeling which hasn't been redeemed, the analysis is stopped, because where there is an emotional bias there is an intellectual blind spot and the analyst can't even see how to go any further with the analysis. This is also a great metaphysical truth. If anything occasions confusion in me, I may gain a little peace, maybe enough to cover some of the confusion, and that is good. However, if we are to become whole, it must be through the *perception of wholeness.* The mold which we create with the intellect, I believe in, and is necessary, but the realization, that which catches fire from Heaven, has to be *like* Heaven. We are reluctant, however, to surrender the fear. There is a certain sense of morbidity in it which we seem to enjoy; there is a certain strange masochistic delight in self-torture. It stems from the race conscious belief that God is against us, and we must be redeemed from it. How, or when, or to what degree, I do not know, but no one has the power to give you life but yourself. The "Bhagavad Gita" says, "The self must raise the self by the self," and Shakespeare said, "To thine own self be true, and it shall follow as the night the day, thou can'st not then be false to any man."

Our work is simple. Sometimes we use big words and indulge in involved discussions, but do not let them confuse you. The universe is simple if we will learn the key. "As above, so beneath; as below, so above; what is true on one plane is true on all." The impulsion is love, the propulsion is law.

In absolute Reality the Spirit that we are looking for is the mind that looks for it! It couldn't be otherwise, for there would be nothing in us capable of knowing It when we see It. In other words, that which you now call your conscious awareness, or your objective mind, is the Spirit functioning at that level of awareness; that which is called the Cosmic consciousness is this same Mind becoming aware at the point of individuality. The reaction to this awareness creates an atmospheric field around the individual. This field, however, also partakes of the nature of the collective psychic field, which has been called the "collective unconscious" or "race mind," and brings into the creative power of Mind—there is only one creative power—what all the world has believed and pushes it out into objective experience because the Law is One. It is as though we went out to homestead an acre of land in virgin country. Someone in authority has divided the land into a thousand acres, and says, "Your number is one thousand and so your acre is the one marked one thousand. It has a fence around it and is of a different color but you may raise what you want to in it. All the soil is the same. The sun, rain, air, and creative fertility is the same, but each of you may have an individual garden. After we have cultivated our individual gardens, let's take all the fences down." After many years of cultivating our individual gardens, what will we find? This can be likened to the span of human existence. We will find much in our own garden that we didn't plant. We might think that the "devil" put it there or that some previous strange experience we had never heard of caused it. Then we find that there are certain similar plants growing in our neighbor's garden that he didn't want and doesn't think he planted. It was all blown in by the wind and dropped by the birds! I do not believe evil belongs to anyone, and we should impersonalize it in our thinking as quickly as we can!

After taking the fences down from around our individual plots we discover that there is only one field. We were all *using* the *same* field! Then I suppose someone realizes the truth and says, "Well, I don't think I planted this. If I did, I was foolish. I will pull out every plant that I do not want, and I will plant only that which I know to be good and which I desire. I will put up a screen so that the wind and the birds no longer drop the seeds I do not want, and I will no longer allow this to happen." It is very good to be specific in certain matters!

If each of us should plant and cultivate a beautiful garden of mind and then were to take all the fences down, we would discover that we were merely individualizing a Universality. There is no such thing as individual psyche, mind, body, or spirit! There is only ONE. The premise is simple and let us keep it that way.

The Law of Mind reacts because it is its nature to do so. We can't change it. However, if we have enough bigness and enough receptivity; if we have enough joy, enough love, enough laughter, enough song; if we have that which is beyond tolerance and charity to downright understanding so that we can say, without lying, ''I behold in thee the image of Him who died on the tree,'' then the dead will rise!

Let us again turn to that divine and radiant center of life, the light that lights every man's path, and consciously identify ourselves with the great love, wisdom and power of the eternal One.

Infinite love within me, which is God, free from all hurt; infinite peace within me, which knows no disturbance or fear; infinite good, ''I am that which thou art, thou art that which I am'' and so unleash, unloose, unstop, and unbind me until at last I know I am free. And so it is.

God of the sun and the rain, the wind, the open air and these mountain peaks; God of our own life, here in the majesty of nature, proclaiming the strength of the Infinite, we indraw thy Divine Breath.

E.H.

Into your heavenly loneliness
　　Ye welcomed me, O solemn peaks!
And me in every guest you bless
　　Who reverently your mystery seeks.
And up the radiant peopled way
　　That opens into worlds unknown,
It will be life's delight to say,
　　'Heaven is not heaven for me alone.'
Rich by my brethren's poverty!
　　Such wealth were hideous! I am blest
Only in what they share with me,
　　In what I share with all the rest.*

*From "Shared" by Lucy Larcom

CHAPTER TWO

Man's Individuality and Identity

eligious Science is based on a very few simple and fundamental ideas. The basic proposition is that the universe in which we live is a combination of Love and Law, or Divine Presence and Universal Principle. We may call it a spontaneous Self-emergence and a mechanical reaction, or the Law and the Word, or the Personal and the Impersonal, or the Thing and the way It works. Everything we do, say, and teach; our methods of treatment and procedures; all is based not on a duality but on a dual unity or a two-sided unity of one and the same thing.

There is the Law and the Word, the breath and the power, the principle and the performance, or the spontaneous self-emergence which is the personal element, and the way it works which is the impersonal. The result of this two-sided unity is life as we see it. This concept is basic to every great philosophy the world has ever known. I am not talking about religious theologies for they are mostly dogmas.

It is basic to our philosophy that we are surrounded by an Infinite Presence and that we are also surrounded by an Infinite Principle, and we never mistake the Principle for the Presence, or the Presence for the Principle. I do not think that a spiritual mind treatment is an intercession on the behalf of any individual. Instead, it is a recognition of man's nature as complying with the Original Nature, and the automatic and mechanical reaction to this recognition is the manifestation of this Nature at the level of our recognition.

This brings us to the proposition that a perception, a recognition or a realization of the undivided Universality necessitates the recognition of the manifestation of the undivided Universality in infinite variations of individualizations of Itself. This is something we cannot avoid. By the same token, a recognition of the true meaning of individualization will give rise to the recognition of Universality. When we understand these things we shall find that our relationship is that of an individualization *in* a Universality, which individualization, becoming *aware* of its Universal Nature, has the infinite possibility of limitless expansion but never the possibility of infinite absorption either by the road of the Universality or by the road of the individualization. If awareness came by the pathway of the Universality, we would be absorbed in the Infinite, which we are not. We are never going to be lost in God but found in God.

On the other hand, if the individualization absorbed the Infinite and the pathway became complete, and the individual became an "eternal" being, he would be on the pathway of everlasting ennui or boredom. Therefore, we have to suppose an Infinite Reality that is neither lost in Its creation nor does It absorb the creation in Itself to the loss of the creation. Rather, the creation eternally expands into the Infinite without actually becoming the Infinite and exhausting the Infinite.

In this we have a two-sided play upon life, of life upon itself. The first of which, we will say, looses the infinite libido, or desire, or craving, which seems to be instinctive in everything as self-expression because all creation exists for the delight of God, not for the salvation of the created. This is where theology is confused. The idea that we exist for the glory of God because God has to have somebody to glorify Him or It, or the idea that we exist that we may come into salvation—both ideas are invalid philosophically. The finite sense of boredom, and the idea of sin and salvation are but the two ends of one morbid illusion. The concept, however, of Infinite Being by Its very nature having irresistible desire and necessity to express Itself that It may come into the fruition of Its self-awareness, and beholds in that which It does that which It is, is necessary to creation.

Personally, I doubt very much if there is any such thing as an infinite abstraction. By that I mean that I do not believe there is any God that knows you beyond your ability to know yourself in God. Otherwise, where would be the you that is known or the God that knows you? This in no way limits the God that knows you, nor does it make you God. Rather, it makes your evolution and mine an ascending scale of self-awareness of that which of Itself does not evolve within Itself, but which evolves everything around It. As I once wrote, "Hid within all things evolved in silence, beauty, wisdom, and will, is that which makes the cycle move, unmove, immovable and still." This is what is meant by "going into the silence," or becoming "quiet."

Yesterday several of us drove up the mountain to Huntington Lake. On the way we paused behind the power plant situated below the lake and watched the water leave the plant and rush down the river. The water, falling by its own weight, obeying gravitational force, creates a natural energy which the generator converts into a usable power. The generator doesn't create, it generates. It takes out the natural energy and transmutes it into a form of power which is distributed over power lines down to the valley and, in turn, drives machinery to do specific things. We can liken this operation to the Cosmic Force, which would be the lake and which exists, at least on the surface, in a state of calm. Out of Its meditation, we will say, comes the movement which expresses as manifestation. This is the Infinite in action. It is true that all nature teaches us the Nature of God, because nature is God manifest.

We have to suppose an infinite self-existent, self-knowing, undivided, indivisible, equally distributed Omnipresence. We may call it God. If we do suppose such an undivided Omnipresence and we consider ourselves in It, then we can only know It as ourselves at the level of our knowledge of It. "As thou seest, that thou beest." I believe the nature of the universe is this way; that there is the Infinite self-existence; this means that there is something that you accept which you can't explain. We never try to explain the inexplicable. Even God could not tell you why God is God, because the God who would be telling you why, the God who would be speaking as God, would not then be self-existent, but would be the God who is in relationship to the Self-Existence. The God that *is* knows only the "is-ness" of Itself. We must be a part of this knowingness, for it is impossible that we could be anything else.

The ancient Hindus, who were very clear thinkers, taught a concept of God that our Bible and every great spiritual system teaches. They taught that the infinite being of God, the Divine Nature, not by will or purpose or plan, is such that It must express Itself because It couldn't come to know Itself other than through Its self-expression. No real thinker has ever taught a divine purpose or a divine plan. All, however, have taught the idea of divine patterns. They have taught that by a process of involution or "the impregnation of the mundane clod" there is involved and invoked a seed of the

Divine Nature which some day shall bear complete proof of Cosmic Being Itself, but it will always be an individualization.

This seed or spark of life, out of the necessity of its nature, goes through all the processes of evolution which are already involved within it. The involution is spontaneous; the evolution is mechanical.

God doesn't plan things, God *is* all that is. An infinite purpose is a mathematical, logical, philosophical, and a spiritual contradiction! Therefore, by reason of the very nature of Reality it is necessary that the Divine impregnates the human and lets it alone to discover itself; however, the human is still subject to the law of its being. The New Testament says, in effect, "If there had been any law under grace whereby man could have been saved by grace"—that is, with experience—"verily through grace such a law would have been given." This means that even if the Infinite could have thought up a way of creating a mechanical spontaneity, then the Infinite would have done it, but even the Infinite cannot do that which contradicts Its nature. There is no law under grace whereby freedom could have been provided automatically except through instinctive, spiritual impregnation and then left alone to discover itself.

"The law was given by Moses but grace and truth came by Christ," said John. Even God could not have created a perfected man to function on this plane because such a man would be an automaton. Therefore, man must go through the experiences of evolution.

This involution and the evolutionary process is the significance of the story of the Garden of Eden. In this story God created Adam and Eve and put them in the garden with the tree of the knowledge of good and evil and said, in effect, "You can eat everything else but if you eat the fruit of this tree, it will be bad because you will become as one of us and live forever." What does that mean? It sounds like a jealous God. Not at all. Some writer was explaining the impossibility of there being anything other than the spontaneous emergence of Spirit. The law already *is* and is the servant of the Spirit throughout the ages, and so man is forbidden to eat of the tree of the knowledge of good and evil lest he become "as one of us and live forever." In other words, there is no such thing as an infinite dualism. You can "eat" of the experience only to the point where the experience determines the need of a new one!

It was inevitable that Adam should eat the fruit and that Eve should have given it to him. In the story Adam and Eve represent the two principles in man; one consciously determines and the other acts as though the determination is true. Eve ate first of the forbidden fruit and then gave it to Adam. Psychology says that wherever there is an emotional bias there is an intellectual blind spot, which means exactly the same thing.

Adam and Eve is just a story about a man who was cast out of the garden and told to make his living by the sweat of his brow but was also told that some day he could return. This may be likened to the journey of the soul, which is necessary. The ancient Hindus called it "the great ignorance." Unfortunately we call it "the fall of man" and give it theological connotations, as though God had cast man out of the Garden of Eden. This is a foolish concept for as soon as the fall has taken place the redemption has to begin, and so we have the journey from Adam to Christ. "For as in Adam all die, even so in Christ shall all be made alive." The first man on this earth to the last man is the "Lord from Heaven."

The ancient Jews had three Adams; the Adam of the earth, the Adam of the air, and the Adam of the sky. One was the tree of life, as the ancient Hindus taught, with the branches pointing downward; the other tree is rooted in the earth with its branches going upward, and where the two meet in the sky there is the coming together of the Universal and the Individual, not to the extinction or accentuation of the Individual, but to the realization of the Universal. In the union the Individual does not become absorbed but is consciously immersed.

> Oh, within all things and around them, Brahma,
> Life of Life Divine,
> Shadow all our days of dreaming
> And solve our being into Thine.
> Rob the mind of its illusions,
> Strip the ego naked bare,
> 'Til the waiting hearts within us
> Find Thy Presence hidden there.
> Let us then awake to union
> That we no more separate be,
> That the Life which seems divided
> Be not lost but found in Thee.

Those are the last three verses of a poem I wrote about Brahma after reading the "Bhagavad Gita" and being impressed with its great beauty.

The "great ignorance" of the ancient Hindus and the "fall of man" of Christian theology based on the story of the Garden of Eden imply that in the process of evolution when the "first saint turns from the clod" there must start the journey of the individualization to Universality, in complete ignorance of itself but never entirely forgetting, as Wordsworth said, "that celestial palace from whence it came." He described the journey this way—"in a season of calm weather (which is meditation), tho' inland far we be (in materiality), our souls have sight of that immortal sea which brought us hither, can in a moment travel thither and see the children sport upon the shore, and hear the mighty waters rolling evermore.'' This is his testimony to the feeling he had toward the Spirit, which never leaves us without a witness.

We are in that process of evolution where it is inevitable that that part of our nature, as represented by Eve, which is that part of us which can be fooled, and which the ancients called ''Maya'' or the illusion of mind, may produce an equal illusion, as represented by Adam. The ancients believed in both a mental and a physical illusion, one as the complement of the other. Eve tempts Adam and then they both have to leave the celestial garden. This starts the whole process of redemption or salvation, or as the ancients called it, ''from ignorance to enlightenment and awakening.'' Emerson said ''there is no sin but ignorance and no salvation but enlightenment'' for ''the finite alone has wrought and suffered, the infinite lies stretched in smiling repose.''

But now let us pass over all the processes, all the stories that every Bible has taught, and consider only the awakening of the universal generic Christ, which, we will say in every day language, is the God-intended man or God's idea of Himself as us. God sees me only to the extent that the Christ in me recognizes Itself as more than human; there is always the evidence of the tree that grew down, growing up, one overshadowing the other. It is destined that the branches shall meet and merge and that the dualism shall become complete unity.

The perception of Universality, the indivisible Oneness of all life, gives us the perception of nearness, of closeness, and if we suppose, as we must, that the Infinite is the Infinite Knower, then we must suppose that this Infinite Oneness and Closeness is the Knower acting through us, around us, about us and within us. In other words, the highest God and the innermost God is the One God, but we do not believe that man is in a thinking union with God.

Eckhart said that the search after union is not union but that when union is complete the search is not only over, it is even forgotten. This is the only process by which and through which the proclamation shall come: "I am that I am besides which there is none other." Eckhart also said, "God never had but one son but the Infinite is forever begetting this only begotten son and he is begetting him in me now." We can see this all about us in nature. We can see that no two blades of grass are alike and yet they are blades of grass; no two trees are alike and no two people are alike. As we see this, we may come to the understanding that there are generic or cosmic patterns of everything that exists. Within each generic or cosmic pattern is the individualization of the infinite members of the one generic pattern. I am not a monkey, I am a man. A rose is not a cactus. An acorn can only become an oak tree. Everything in the universe is sharply individualized.

Now we have the perception of individualization from the standpoint of Universality. This perception of the Universality, with the necessity in Its own being to express, gives us the concept and awareness of the individualization. We have turned our concept around and, from the standpoint of individualization, arrived at the perception and awareness of the universalization. This is the activity of the creative process in the individual. As we put these two great perceptions of Individuality and Universality together we find that they are distinct yet unified, that they are separate without being sep-

41

arated. Without this we would have the concept of individuality as separate from the Infinite, or, if we abstract our thought considerably, we would have a concept of the Universality as the individual, and we would try to play the role of God before we even know how to be an intelligent man.

Man is not God. God is man. All ice is water; some water is ice, but all water is not ice; neither is ice all the water there is. In other words, we must be aware of an inner play of a Universality beyond us, forever extending, widening and deepening our individuality, generically. I think that out of the generic pattern, which is the individuation in the universe, comes the Christ—this is different from Jesus, who was only a type of man who had to come to embody the Christ. Jesus was the human person. We do not deny personality but we do affirm individuation of Universality. To me that is very important. There are too many metaphysicians who say you must not be a *person*. You can't help being a person! How are you and I going to blot out what the Almighty did? There is nothing wrong with personality because it is the *echo* of the individuation. It is wrong only when it is separated from itself, divided against itself or psychically multiplied against itself. We should have more personality, but we do not develop it by studying to be dynamic, but rather by listening and knowing the generic pattern or idea which is back of it, the Christ, the Universal individuation.

If you are shocked by what I say, you will have to stop thinking the way you do because that kind of religious thinking is merely another kind of disease, and we are not going to create a new disease out of our philosophy. This whole thing we are talking about is the emergence of life in us. It is what makes us sing and dance, and love, and create, and be born in this world and then die to it; all of which is a natural process, not as an evolution of the Spirit Itself, because It is an eternal changelessness, but the evolution of that nature which expresses, without which even God would not "know." We are the self-knowingness of God at the level of whatever we are. The New Testament writer said that if there had been any law under grace whereby the love of God could have given freedom then verily by grace or love such a law would have been given, and he went on to say that we have always been and will be under the law of bondage until the advent of Christ.

Isaiah said, "He leads captivity captive." This is one of the most beautiful and powerful concepts in the Bible. It means that the law is our servant leading us to Christ; Christ redeems us from the law. In the same passage he goes on to say, "Is the law then of no avail? God forbid." He perceived, as we must, that without being a duality, the universe is, in this sense, a dual unity. Browning said the same thing when he said, "All is love, yet all is law."

Judge Troward, when speaking of the Law and the Word, said that the sequence of the creative order starts with absolute intelligence, which thinks, or moves, or invokes itself, and is the Word. Out of this, for its expression, the law is created and then the thing. So we have intelligence, word, law, and the thing, in a descending scale of the evolutionary process, which is the creative process in the individual.

The New Testament writer said that there was no law under grace to provide freedom, and that even love couldn't have done it. Even God cannot do that which is not God. Therefore, he stated that the law came by Moses, but grace came by Christ; Isaiah prophesied that captivity shall be led

43

captive. This means that the law which Moses taught, the law the ancients taught—Karma, the law of cause and effect—is not a lie, and we will never escape it, but now it will be a servant and not a master! This is the final consummation of the creative process which began endless eons ago to produce individuation in Universality without denying the one or blotting out the other.

Man will never absorb God and God will never absorb man. If either took place, both would become instantly extinct. Should man absorb God, the finite would have long ago eaten up the Infinite and that is impossible. The finite would have exhausted the possibility of the Infinite without arriving at an eternal experience. We can never exhaust the inexhaustible. If, on the other hand, through annihilation the Infinite could absorb the finite, the Infinite Itself would no longer be expressed and It would become non-existent, which is impossible and unthinkable. There is no such thing as a consciousness which is not conscious, nor an awareness that isn't aware. Psychology defines self-awareness as the emergence through the creative reproductive urge of the emotional nature of love in the human being; and states that the first law of self-awareness is that the libido must have an object; the ego must not be rejected. This is fundamental to the emotional life of everything on earth. Why? Because everything is made of the One Cosmic Nature.

We cannot countenance the Buddhist's idea of absorption. Sri Aurobindo wrote in the "Divine Life," which is one of the great books of modern times, that "Buddhism is annihilism." I have known it since I first studied Buddhism, but I never thought anyone would have the nerve to say it, analyzing it the way he did to prove it. He said that this concept is annihilistic because it teaches the absorption of the ego into the Universality, this being exactly what the evolutionary process does not do. Instead, the Universality seeks to create through the irresistibility of an inner impulsion, not by plan, or purpose, or will, but by nature. Do you know what the difference is? This means that the individual, what Aurobindo called the gnostic man, will in a sense be the Infinite without absorbing the Infinite, and without extincting any other individual, come to understand and know Him.

Let us suppose that the processes of evolution and creation created the hills, you and me, and everything else; that we have gone through "the fall," eaten of the fruit of the knowledge of good and evil, and we have had a "hell" of a time and here we are! It is the only "hell" we will ever know and we are overcoming it, but I do admit that we have had a "hell" of a time! If someone were to ask me if I believe in a hell, I would say "no" but I believe in "hells." We have all been through them and we know it. None of them were real and yet they were less than something but more than nothing! They were not imposed upon us by the universe but by the necessity of our own experience. Browning said, "then welcome each rebuff that turns earth's smoothness rough." We do not always welcome them but we will have these experiences until we learn how futile they are.

Let us say that the Infinite creation in its Infinite process has arrived at the point, humanly speaking, where It has become something that knows, or thinks Itself as separate from everything else; at least It knows that It is not a tree.

A fire-mist and a planet,
    A crystal and a cell,
A jellyfish and a saurian,
    And caves where the cave-men dwell;
Then a sense of law and beauty,
    And a face turned from the clod,—
Some call it Evolution,
    And others call it God. *

This creation has come to the point of self-discovery and is naming everything, yet is afraid of everything around it, because it doesn't know it is one with everything. We have been through all these processes of evolution and so let us forget them, for they are not essential now. We are like the woman who said she was so thirsty and someone got her a drink of water and then asked if she felt better and she said, "Yes, but I was *so* thirsty!" Troward said, "A neurotic thought pattern repeats itself with monotonous regularity throughout life." But now we have come to the point of self-discovery and have been through the process.

Now, what is our teaching of evolution going to be in comparison with what it has been? It is going to be this—through identification comes the reciprocal action which flows through the instrument and brings forth into our world, and the world around us, that which is higher, finer and better. If it is true that you and I are God at the level of what we are, we only *think* the tree is outside of us. We shouldn't be conceited about this and strut around saying, "I am God." Many people do it and their trouble is psychic, or a certain form of confusion, and yet their claim is true if they knew what it meant, which most of them don't. God doesn't go

---

*"Each in His Own Tongue," by William Herbert Carruth

around screaming, "I am God." However, it must be that the reciprocal action would have to come from conscious identification, because the unconscious has done all it could by arbitrary methods, for had there been any great law, under grace, whereby it could be done by an outside agency, to lead captivity captive and enable us to express ourselves, it would have been established. Jesus said, in effect, "Who shall tell me that I shall not do it; which one of you condemns me?" And he said, "You haven't a bit of power to do so."

Our evolution from now on will have to be through our conscious identification, through personal choice and volition. "I am That" and as I *know* I am That, then "That" is knowing Itself at the level of my knowing that "I am That." It is the meaning of the great "Thou I" and the great "I Thou." Also, "I am that which thou art, thou art that which I am," or "I am that I am, besides which there is none other." The two are one in the subtle sense that the Infinite forever flows through the finite. Emerson wrote, "There is a place for all of It," and added, "sometimes the muse too strong for the bard sits astride his neck and writes through his hand." We all shall have to come to the point of conscious identification, setting up the reciprocal action at a higher level. "*As* I see It, It sees me!"

Please remember that I am not saying there is no law. If there were no law, there would be no cosmos. There is law everywhere present. The law is, however, the servant of the Eternal Spirit, and all sequences of cause and effect become the tools of God and man. This is what laws were intended to be and they become so through the ascending scale of recognizing more and more of That which *is*. However, we must loose our littleness in the process. There is a peak somewhere that overlooks every other peak. Every peak that is less than

47

that highest peak will obstruct the view back of that peak even while we look at it. This is true symbolism. Even our vision of God can obstruct God until we see as God sees!

In the higher identification there is some mountaintop which overlooks all the others. In Bunyan's story "Pilgrim's Progress," he wrote, "as he made the ascent the burden dropped from his shoulders." There are no burdens "up there," for as Emerson said, "The finite alone has wrought and suffered, the infinite lies stretched in smiling repose." It is our purpose in teaching and practice to individualize the Universal, and through individualizing the Universal to universalize the individual!

Infinite Spirit within us, Eternal Presence, Holy of Holies, heart of every heart, pulsing, vibrating, indwelling, "I am that which thou art, thou art that which I am." When this material universe shall be rolled up like a scroll and numbered with the things that were once thought to be, I am.

"The Lord is in His Holy Temple, let all the earth be silent before Him." Be silent all ignorance, all fear, all doubt, all pain! We are identifying ourselves with the living Spirit and "that which thou art, art that which I am" as eternal wholeness and happiness.

Let the song be full and all the weight and the burden fall backwards as we face the sun!

"O living Truth that shall endure when all that seems shall suffer shock, rise on the rock and make us pure."

Amen.

Infinite God within and around us, we feel Thy Presence in our souls.

There is One Life, which is God; One perfect Presence, which is good; besides which there is nothing else no matter what appears to be. This ONE we accept.

In the beauty and wholeness which surrounds us; in the midst of this "peace which passeth all understanding"—

G.M.

Our Father which art in Heaven,
Hallowed be thy name.
Thy kingdom come.
Thy will be done in earth, as it is in Heaven.
Give us this day our daily bread.
And forgive us our debts, as we forgive our debtors.
And lead us not into temptation, but deliver us from evil:
For thine is the kingdom, and the power, and the glory,
    for ever.   Amen.

CHAPTER THREE

The Past and Future are Now

ertain phases of immortality interest me more and more. We are often apt to think of immortality as the continuity of the individual life from the standpoint that we die here and become alive somewhere else! This is true in a sense, but I do not want to die before I become alive! This is the general belief about immortality, but I do not believe immortality is this way.

We are living in a timeless universe; a universe where time is merely a measure of experience. St. Augustine said, "Time is a sense of recollection and anticipation." Dean Inge said, "Time is a measure in a unitary wholeness." So we can say that time is any measure of experience. Time is *of* creation and not a thing in itself. There would be no such thing as time unless there were something to experience it. Infinite time is not something experienced separate from Infinite Being but is the manifestation of Infinite Being. Therefore, to wait for that time when we are to become immortal is to wait for that which is philosophically, logically, and mathematically impossible. That is why John said, "Beloved, now are we the sons of God, and it doth not yet appear what we shall be, but we know that, when he shall appear, we shall be like him; for we shall see him as he is."

Analyzing this statement, we find we are now the sons of God but it doesn't appear what we really are, and we do not know what we shall be like but when "he" shall appear we shall be like Him. He shall have to *appear* in order for us to see Him and to discover we are like Him when we see Him, but we shall not discover this until we see Him *as He is*. We know that when He shall appear we shall be like Him *because* we shall see *Him* as He is, and when we see Him as He is we shall be like that which we see. "Beloved, now are we the sons of God," but it does not yet appear until we wake up!

This isn't complicated; it is very simple. "Surely goodness and mercy shall follow me all the days of my life and I shall dwell in the house of the Lord forever," is just another way to say it. Or, indubitably, benignity and commiseration shall pursue me all the diurnity of my vitality and I shall externalize my habitation in the metropolis of nature, is the same thing in different words!

The prophet said, "Awake thou that sleepest, and arise from the dead, and Christ shall give thee light." Throughout the Bible and in all the other great Bibles of the world there is this idea. The whole concept of our Bible, and every Bible I have ever read, is that we are asleep to something to which we should awake, to something which is not asleep, and to which of necessity we shall awaken, for as Browning said, we shall "fall from the dream of probation to find ourselves bathed in new life," and we shall remember "in glory, ere error had bent the broad brow from the daily communion." In other words, we go from the physical to the mental to the spiritual pattern.

That we will remember who we are and what we are, I am certain. When Saul, in Browning's poem "Saul," reached this discovery "he slowly resumed his old motions and habitudes kingly." Then the story relates that David goes on in the night, pretty much like we are in this great mountain vastness, and is surrounded by witnesses, which Browning called "the alive, the awake, and the aware." This is a perfect thought—that which is alive, that which is aware, and that which is awake!

Every bible rightly interpreted teaches us that we are asleep to something to which we would awake; that we are dead and should become resurrected; that every moment of our existence is a fresh beginning; that every day is the world made new, and that there is nothing in the universe which retards our evolution but our own ignorance. Emerson said "there is no sin but an ignorance, and no salvation but enlightenment." He also said that we are gods on a debauch and that once in awhile we all wake up and look around us but we very soon sink back into the hypnosis from which we have awakened. Though we are all hypnotized from the cradle to the grave, some of us do wake up once in awhile to some great harmony, to some great truth, to some great beauty, and with a sneaking glance we see something we do not see in ordinary moments; and this is not insanity because the more we see this thing the more real it becomes. I am not speaking about psychic phenomena but about spiritual illumination. There is a vast difference.

It is very interesting to me that when they told Jesus that Lazarus was dead, he said, "I go to awaken him." When he arrived at the cemetery he found certain obstructions. There was the tomb, the stone in front of the tomb, the family standing around weeping and wailing, the conventions, and back of all that was what Jung called "the collective unconscious," which the Bible calls "the carnal mind," which is what everyone believes about a man when he is dead. Jesus, however, said, "I have come to awaken him; roll away the stone." Then he stepped up before the tomb and said, "Father, I thank thee that thou hast heard me." That was the unification, the recognition, the identity. "And I know that thou hearest me always," which was further unification and agreement. Next, he used the authority of the law of which he had become aware and said, "Lazarus, come forth."

Immortality is not something we are going to wait for. I have never conducted a funeral without announcing that we believe in immortality, which of course we do, and in the continuity and the ongoing of the individual soul from wherever it left to wherever it is going. There cannot be any breach, for then there would be an amnesia, and there could not be such a thing as this in Spirit. I also believe that all persons are immortal or no person is immortal! There is always someone who suspects the corpse, you know! None of us are so good that we can make ourselves immortal beings, and by the same token none of us are so bad that we can destroy our immortality! Jesus understood this.

Moses and the ancient Hindus taught the karmic law of cause and effect. Moses said it would be visited unto the third and fourth generations for those who hate God, and the people who believed seriously in this law believed that for what has happened, you will pay the utmost farthing, an eye for an eye and a tooth for a tooth. I do not believe in it for it seems to me that it is a tremendous limitation to impose on infinity. This was a great teaching, however, for it represents the balance and equilibrium of the universe, which equals Einstein's first equation where he said that everything bends back upon itself—time, light, and space. Thus, the Infinite can be described as a circle, having neither beginning nor end. As Inge said, "you cannot have an infinity described by a straight line, because it supposes itself to be cut off at both ends." Einstein mathematically reiterates in his first equation what

THE PAST AND FUTURE ARE NOW

all the great teachers have told us: "as a man sows, so shall he also reap," or "he who loses his life shall find it," or as Whitman said, "the gift is most to the giver and comes back most to him."

We cannot dissolve the law of cause and effect. The law *is*. Moses taught this law as a ruthless law. Jesus, however, said, "I am not come to destroy, but to fulfill." What was it Jesus added to this teaching that the Hindus and the ancient Hebrews hadn't taught? He added a personal factor to the impersonal law, and this is one of the great steps forward in human thought. This personal factor is the greatest single value in the Christian faith.

I do not believe that Christians should be dogmatic. Christianity hasn't done such a good job, you know. Most of the modern wars have been waged among the Christians. Christianity has never really been tried and no one really knows if it will work. With logical reasoning we could see that it would work if it were tried. It is a pretty tough proposition to be a Christian. It is tough because there are certain things we have to believe, and as they say in modern psychology, self-awareness is not enough, we must *do* things. "If ye know these things, happy are ye if ye do them."

The theory is easy but we have to practice the principles and that is difficult to do. It is easy to tell other people what to do. Who is there among us who does love his neighbor as himself? Who has lost all of his pride? Who has lost all of his curse? Who has lost all of his nakedness? Who has lost every capacity to hurt anything in the universe? He alone at that point shall reach his salvation and discover himself as he was before he woke up, and he is that now. We are all somewhere on the pathway. Jesus knew this and said that he had not come to destroy but to fulfill the law, and he added what we may call the personal factor—that at any given moment the great law of cause and effect may be intercepted and reversed by the volition of the personal element.

This is the greatest thing for us to learn. It is the Law in which we believe in conjunction with the Spirit which we adore, commune with, reverence and worship. This is why Jesus told the parable of the man that came in at the eleventh hour. He said the same thing to the man on the cross beside him, "today thou shalt be with me in Paradise." Jesus didn't say it because the man had said to him, "I am no good and now I know you are my Lord Jesus." The man wasn't a religious person.

When Jesus said, "he who loses his life will find it," he was announcing that no matter what happened yesterday, today, in one split second, it may all be changed if we will but let it be changed. However, we cannot carry along today the corpse of yesterday and expect the change to take place, and this is our trouble. We love the idea of the resurrection but it is very difficult for us to unwrap the grave clothes of our previous experience. It used to be said "that man is a sinner and he will get his later on!" How do we know? The only hell there is, that I ever expect to experience, is in my own mind and I am gradually overcoming it and it is hot enough!

Are we willing to let go? Nearly every day I talk with someone who has lost a friend, a husband or a wife, or someone betrayed him. My answer is, so what? That is human experience and to err is human. Are you now going to carry this corpse around with you? I say to these women who are left alone—why don't you go out into society and see what you can do for yourself? To me that isn't silly. People are missing companionship terribly because they carry around this dead body —somebody betrayed us, someone lied to us, someone died.

Last Saturday, as I was driving here, a young fellow hailed me. He had just been released from the Army and wanted to get to San Diego. I picked him up and we began talking. After about a half hour's conversation, I said to myself, "This boy has had a bad background. He hates his father and I think maybe he hates his mother, and he sees them in everyone he meets. He is even suspicious of me. Why did I pick him up?"

Presently I said, "I'm hungry. Let's stop and get a sandwich." I wanted to talk with him more and see if I was right.

After we were seated in the restaurant and the waitress had taken our order, I said, "Isn't she a sweet girl?"

He answered, "Yes, but she doesn't like me."

I asked, "Why doesn't she like you?"

He replied, "She thinks she is better than I am."

I said, "Let me ask you something. Did you like your father and mother?"

And he said, "My old man was no good and my mother was worse." It developed that his parents had been married just a week before his birth, and there was the picture.

I asked him how old he was and he replied, "Twenty-one." Then I asked him, "Do you want to be unhappy all your life?" He, of course, said, "No," and then I asked him, "Do you know what a corpse is?"

He replied, "Well, of course; I've seen plenty of them in Korea."

I replied, "How would you like to go around all the rest of your life with a corpse tied to your back?" He thought that was a crazy question and told me so, saying, "I wouldn't talk like that; what are you, anyway?"

I answered, saying, "Oh, I'm a preacher."

"Nuts, preachers don't talk the way you talk."

"Well," I replied, "I don't know; that is one of those things that cannot be answered by 'yes' or 'no', isn't it?"

The boy said, "Well, I hadn't thought of that."

I continued, "How would you like to carry a corpse? How would you like to have six corpses on your back?" Of course he said, "That's impossible!" But I told him, "You've already told me you are carrying around two; one is your mother and the other is your father, and now you are gathering them up along the roadside everywhere you go. How can you stand it? What is going to happen to a fellow like you? Don't you want to be happy?"

He said "yes" to that question, and I think his whole experience is going to be changed. I told him in effect to "wake up, get somewhere, don't go around fighting the world. You've just been having the wrong idea about yourself." He is going to wake up and that's a resurrection, but he cannot be resurrected from his sense of inferiority without letting go of those things which made it.

A great many people have a big superiority complex, which is merely an inferiority complex whistling to keep up its courage! I told the boy that I was a certain kind of a minister and he asked what kind. I told him that I didn't like any of the religions I was acquainted with and so I had made up one that I did like. He thought that was crazy, and it does sound that way, but if you studied history you would find that this is the way all religions are founded. Each is just a new version of the old, and people will call the new one "odd" for awhile, like a new style, but bye and bye everyone accepts it. This is literally true. This is the way all of our religions or theologies have been started. This is the way we get our words; somebody has to make them up. God doesn't have a fountain pen and write in a ledger and drop the leaves of it on the hilltop!

We say that the mountains show forth the glory of God but it isn't that way. The mountains *are* the glory of God in the same sense that Einstein's second equation tells us that energy and mass are equal, identical and interchangeable. This equation is fundamental to our philosophy, for Einstein isn't saying that energy energizes mass. That is exactly what he isn't saying. He is not saying that it flows through and influences and controls mass. He says energy *is* mass. Spinoza said, "Mind and matter are the same thing," and now modern physics is beginning to tell us that the physical universe is but a shadow of some substance which we do not see. These mountains here do not reflect the glory of God, they *are* the glory of God. In other words, there isn't a mountain which God "up there" reflects into a mirror so that we see a mountain "down here." The mountain is God's idea of Himself that way. That is why we can commune with nature in her visible form, and that is why a tree can speak to us, which it most certainly can if we would develop the ability to listen.

We have made the greatest claim upon life of any group of people that has ever lived. I am not speaking of just our small group here, but of those ten or fifteen million people who are making this claim in the different fields of the modern metaphysical movement. We have made the greatest claim upon life and yet we are carrying corpses on our backs. How many? God only knows; hate, viciousness, greed, and the inability to come clean even with each other. A frustrated metaphysician is the most frustrated person who ever lived! Why? Because a psychic frustration calls a halt on one's desires and acceptance and need. Now, that we are making the biggest claim on life and are actually in partnership with the Infinite in a very intimate way, in a personal way, if things do not come right for us, we are going to be terribly disappointed!

I think that the reason circumstances often do not work out right for us is because we don't get out of the way, get our "bloated nothingness out of the way of the divine circuits," as Emerson said. We must dissolve this make-believe ego. I do not mean that we dissolve the reality of the ego, for we do not expect to get lost, rather to be found in God. Sir Rabindranath Tagore in "The Vedanta, the Realization of Individuality," said, "Nirvana is not an abstraction. It isn't being lost but a waking up to discover that we are immersed in the Infinite."

If life has to proceed in a logical sequence until it is changed, and we die physically, nothing will have happened to us except the body corpse that we now see will have been buried. We shall have taken all the other corpses along with us. That is tough to realize, isn't it? We cannot lay these corpses down by our own graveside. We can only lay down the physical one, for nature seems to have provided that when for some reason this physical body is no longer a fit instrument, it must be discarded.

For every death there is a resurrection. This is the way of life; this is the way of evolution. No man can become resurrected to love and carry hate with him. This is absolutely impossible to do even though we convert our old hates into theological ones and condemn others and think they are traveling the wrong road. We shall still have hell attached to our backs and the corpse which goes with it. This is inevitable, for Emerson also said, "the integrity of nature is never violated one iota." It is not only this physical body that has to die but all the other dead corpses, for God is love, givingness, harmony, truth, beauty, wisdom and power.

To what degree are we willing to give up every race prejudice, every thought that sets us apart intellectually and spiritually from others? Also, there is that which is even more difficult: to what extent are we willing to give up our time to serve the corpse? It is so hard to let go of these corpses! Why? Because we haven't sublimated them into the things of reality. We say God is love but how do we know God is love? "Love only knows and comprehendeth love," said Whittier. There is no other way. Are we willing to let go of our animosities, our dislikes? Love cannot occupy the space that we give to disharmony. The two do not meet; they do not mix, and so we must die daily. The cells of our bodies do. They tell us that the cells in our bodies are not the same ones that were there eleven months ago. Then where do the wrinkles come from? What is the trouble?

I think more and more there is no such thing as heart trouble, there is only a troubled heart. There is no such thing as a disease *per se,* it is the end result of what is wrong with the whole world, and I do not believe that even the individual suffers by himself. In the old order they used to say your sins will find you out, and then the new order says, "this man is being tried, error has him." It is a cold-blooded analysis of nothing! Evil doesn't belong to any of us. The lie that a liar tells does not belong to the liar. Even in modern psychiatry they separate the neurosis from the neurotic. We will have to learn to see back of all this kind of thinking to the one central fact which we are trying to comprehend—that there is an evolutionary will pushing us on and upward. There is that something within us, like the prodigal son, that never forgets.

It has given me great gratification recently in reading a number of scientific books to discover that in the new physics they say that while we will still deal with the old physical laws of cause and effect, we know that they are no longer arbitrary, that there is a volitional element that can enter in at any moment. We believe that there is One Presence, One Power, One Mind, One Law, and One Good, and of similar nature is

Einstein's last equation which announces that there is but one physical law governing all other physical laws.

We could create a great religion in pure metaphysics, philosophically and spiritually, out of the findings of three of modern physics' great equations. First, is Einstein's theory of Relativity, that everything bends back upon itself—time, light, and space. This is the law of compensation that circles in spiritual order and includes everything that exists. This is comparable to the karmic law of the East—"as ye sow, so shall ye reap." Next comes Einstein's equation for mass and energy, E equals MC², which means for us that the invisible and the visible are the same. Paul said, "things are not made of the things that do appear." The third equation is Heisenberg's Theory of Indeterminacy, which implies that no matter what happened yesterday it doesn't have to happen tomorrow, but we must first have a clearance of yesterday. This is identical with the teaching of Jesus when he taught the gospel of self-givingness as a complement to the necessity of the divine giving.

We would like to receive the divine giving, but are we willing to let go of everything that inhibits that givingness through us to others? Nothing that we hold, nothing that we keep, nothing that we store up wrapped in the grave clothes of our sense of isolation and separate personality can be anything but a corpse, and we have to stay in the tomb with the corpse! This is our trouble, and I doubt not that all of our disease, all of our accidents, all of hell as we conceive it, and everything that denies the Truth is merely the result of the inability of the individual, and the aggregate of individuals, to let "the dead bury their dead" and step forward in the evolutionary process to carry nothing forward that inhibits the new viewpoint. There should be nothing chaotic in our ability to step forward. Rather, there should be a feeling of ease, and an ever increasing certainty, and we would not pretend that we, as individuals, contain that integrity. There is an integrity greater than our own!

It is very difficult for us to give up our devil and our hell, theologically, but some day it is demanded that we do it in simplicity, because we can't take them to heaven and we can't drag them down to a "hell." Some day we will have to give up and die to everything that is unkind, all manner of conceit, everything that sets ourselves up and causes us to appear in our own imagination, or thought, or will, to be any different from the most degraded soul. If we are to live cosmically, we have to learn this. So, we will have to surrender even the pride of our form of worship. We will have to learn that the man who lies drunk in the gutter and the man who prays in exaltation before the throne of his convictions, "each in his separate star is drawing the things as he sees it from the God of things as they are."

I haven't arrived; you haven't arrived. We are still carrying the corpses of our dead—somebody stole from us, our parents were unkind to us, somebody we loved fell in love with somebody else. If it is true that only the man who loses his life shall find it, he shall not find it all until he has lost it all. That would be a morbid thing if we were thinking of physical death. That hasn't anything to do with it, for people do not die. As far as I know no one has ever died, no matter what his conviction was. He just carried his conviction along with him. Everyone lives forever, and as Browning said, "good will come at last as life to all."

"In my Father's house there are many mansions," said Jesus. We do not have to worry about the integrity of the universe. We do not have to tell God what to do. God has already done it for us but we have failed to accept it because now "we see as through a glass darkly." This is what sin is. It is the great mistake, the consciousness of separation, and we are trying to return to the Father's house. The Father did not condemn the prodigal son. God does not argue! When the boy said, "Dad, I want you to divide my portion," the Father didn't say to him, "Now wait a minute, son, I have only so much and this is your share and you mustn't go over to that place and gamble with it, for that is a bad place!"

The great value to the story is that the Father didn't argue and so the boy went out and spent the money and pawned all his clothes. He was a Jewish boy and finally he got a job feeding the pigs, which is the worst thing that could happen to an orthodox Jew, for they do not even eat pork. "He would fain feed his belly upon the husks that the swine did eat but no man gave unto him." No man ever gives but to himself. Life has made the gift and we are to accept it the way it is made and not some other way. There was that indelible memory, however, within the boy and one day he sat down in the ruin of his life and remembered, as Wordsworth put it, "that celestial palace from whence he came," and said to himself that he would go back, though he knew he wasn't worthy.

The next great point of the story is that the Father sees him afar off—the reciprocal action. It comes to us as we go to It, but we have to leave the pigpen. We have to give up the sense of separation, nor can we carry the consciousness of union other than to inclusion. The boy then threw himself down and said, "Father, I am no longer worthy to be thy son; make me thy hired man," but God didn't even know he was dirty! He just told the boy that he was very glad to see him and took him in and gave him the seamless robe, and the Father brought everyone together and they had a big party.

What is the meaning of this the greatest of all parables? Adela Rogers St. Johns, the writer, said to me recently that it is the greatest story ever told because it has the most human drama in it. It is the greatest spiritual lesson Jesus taught. Why do we not realize that the Father advanced to meet the boy and didn't condemn him? The judgment was gone!

The boy that stayed at home and thought he was a good boy had to get rid of the corpse too. He had left the Father's house but he didn't know it. He had never had a party and when he complained about it, the Father said, "Well, heaven knows there is plenty here to have it with!" Nature turns to us as we turn to it but we have to turn clean. Are you and I carrying corpses? We all are!

Mrs. St. Johns also told me that recently while reading, the word "grievance" came to her attention. She said she hadn't heard nor thought of that word for years and asked herself if she had a grievance. She couldn't think of one relating to the present time but she remembered a time when she associated with a certain group of people in Hollywood. They would gather around at parties and sweetly compliment each other but would be thinking "I never want to see you again." She remembered that she used to think they were saying nothing that she was interested in and that she didn't like them. That was the only grievance she could remember and so she decided to sit right down and dissolve it.

She said to herself, "There is only One, that is God. Everything is all right and whether I ever see these people again or not makes no difference. God is all there is and there isn't anything else, and I will not carry this idea around in my mind any longer." She went out to lunch and when she returned the phone was ringing. When she answered it, the man on the wire said he had been trying to reach her for over an hour and in an apologetic tone of voice asked if she was still angry with him, and she said of course not. Then he went

65

on to say that he had been trying to get up the courage for some time to ask her to write a certain story because he felt there was no one else living who could do it, and she consented to write it. The man, you see, had been a member of the group in Hollywood.

We cannot carry the grievance into the future. It is very, very difficult for us to let go of the corpses. Isn't this a strange state of affairs? A corpse in each hand and more on our back —always the lying, festering corpses! Does not Jung speak of a psychic wound, the psychic fester, and the psychic surgery? Literally, this is true, but Jesus said he who loses his life shall find it. This doesn't mean that we believe in immortality so that when we die we won't have to be afraid of the hereafter. That is the thinking of a craven coward! That is a man who hasn't had sense enough to think it through and to know that there has to be an integrity in the universe. That is the man who hasn't confidence enough in the Thing that put him here to know that It will know what to do with him! You and I do not put anything in anything, we take it all out. Everything! We eat ham sandwiches and mince pie and drink milk and it all turns into hair and blood and bone and muscle, and we do not have anything to do with it!

What is this creative process of nature? If we were in harmony with it, we wouldn't be sick, but how can we be healed if that which causes our disease is a corpse which we will not let go? We can't and we shouldn't try, but rather we should seek a complete clearance. I know of no way to get it other than through a complete surrender to that Power which is greater than we are, and I do not believe that it is to the loss of our individuality but to the discovery of it. I do not believe it is a law which the universe imposes upon us so as to say, "we will show you who is boss around here."

We are a group of people who believe in a truth, which we are endeavoring to prove. What is it? It is that *God is all there is,* not up in the sky but *right here.* God *is* the mountain. Whatever the thing is we call God, there is only that and nothing else from which all is made. When we awake we shall be like Him but *we shall have to see Him as He is,* and not as you and I think He ought to be.

Our thoughts even are not creative, they merely use a creativity.

It seems to me that we are set between the great Omnipresence and the great Omnipotence beholding the face of Him who inhabits eternity. Meister Eckhart said, ''Our work is done better even though our face is turned from our work.'' What does that mean? It means that the greater love includes the lesser. It means to have the perception of love and givingness, and of forgivingness; to be willing to let go of everything no matter if it is something that tickles the morbidity of our affection, because we loved and seemed to have lost. Our trouble isn't in the losing. It is because we built around us an iron dome with one small perforation to let in the only light that there could be, and when that light failed there was no light and how great was the darkness! We have to remove the dome; our love must be expressed for all people. We are afraid to love that much; we are cowards! Why? Because we cannot conceive a love great enough to include all, but we do have the pattern of those few whom we do love.

This is the great challenge set before us, and we have the love and the teachings of Jesus, whom we consider the greatest of the great teachers. We understand the contributions he made to the Hindu and ancient Hebrew philosophies—the ability of the individual at any moment to step

in to intercept, reverse, and place himself in a new relationship to God. "This day shalt thou be with me in Paradise!"

**Now we willingly lay aside everything in the past that hurt
us or that we hurt, and we lift our eyes to that tombless life in
which God is over all, in all, and through all. We surrender
everything that denies its beauty and peace and enjoy the
song and dance of the joy of life. "Thou, which doest all
things divine and fashions for the best, help us to see with
mortal eyes to overlook the rest."**

The Infinite Presence which embraces us within Itself—the eternal God, we recognize as Life, and identify our own with It.

We open our consciousness to the influx of all wisdom and knowledge, knowing that a little child within us shall lead us to the depths and heights, and the width and breadth of that Truth which is perfect. Amen.

G.M.

CHAPTER FOUR

The Universe Is Spiritual Law and Order

The perception of law and order in the universe gives rise, or should give rise, to the authority and the power of prayer, faith and treatment. In metaphysics we have three offices to perform, two in particular. One is to soar in the clouds, courting the mystical element and the intuitive perception, which is beautiful and we all love to do it. We must soar and we must speculate. We draw fire from heaven and we know that God speaks to the heart more than to the intellect.

On the other hand, there comes the time when we must apply these wonderful truths that we know and take them about the highways and byways of life, and we must feel that we have an authority in this activity. I do not think a spiritual mind treatment must be an inspiration. Writers who write commercially, just write. That is their business. Singers who sing commercially, sing, whether they are inspired or not.

One in our field, however, cannot wait for inspiration. It is a mistake to say, "I will give a treatment when I feel like giving a treatment." We do not *feel* like giving a treatment. We *give* a treatment, bringing to bear upon it as much feeling as we can at any particular time.

Our work is not an activity wherein we lose ourselves, either in the mysticism of the spiritual realm or the too often psychic hallucination of the subjective realm. Rather, we perceive that the universe is a combination of Spirit and law and order and that one is the complement of the other. Our perception that the universe has this dual reality, or unity, brings the inspiration of the Spirit directly, extending through man, to that which is to be accomplished on earth. We do not say, let God do it, in the sense that God will bake the biscuits! We say, let God do it, only in the sense that God is all there is, or, let the God in me do it. In other words, a metaphysician is not one, in my estimation, who says that people are not sick or hungry, poor, weak or unhappy, or that they are not born in this world and die to it. Rather, he is one, it seems to me, who includes all that *is* in what is—the ups and downs, the good and bad, without ever having to admit that there is any final dualism, any final evil, or any final problem of the Spirit. Problems are of the mind!

We perceive that the universe is a thing of beauty, of love. I believe that the impulsion of the universe is love and its propulsion is law, and one balances the other. It is inconceivable that it could be otherwise. One is personal, the other is impersonal. It seems to me that we are dealing with something that starts with pure intelligence. When the movement of this intelligence, which we call thought or contemplation, blends its specialization of law through a particular phase or mode of thought, it creates in a certain sense the law of its own being out of the law of all Being. This law, being the movement of intelligence and creativity, carries with it by the nature and constitution of its own being, and the Being of self-existence upon which it relies, everything necessary to impel and propel itself into action. For us it will be action through us. Therefore, the Law set in motion produces the result.

I believe that no matter how much we shall love—and we do not love enough for love is the impulsion—that love alone, as a mere sentiment, will not do anything. For instance, to say, "God is all there is" is not a spiritual mind treatment. It is a statement of our conviction. Too many people think it is a treatment. It is only when we apply our *concept* of the Allness and the Isness of the Beingness of this One Power, it is only when we distribute the power definitely toward a concrete manifestation, or become aware of the Spirit in such a way that it automatically and impersonally reflects in our environment, helping everything it touches, that we become the instrument for that with which we have identified the mind. We have these two great realities, identification and instrumentality.

If law obtains in the universe and is the government of everything, which it most certainly is, then law is of itself and in itself impersonal and neutral. It has no offices to perform of itself but must be stimulated or impregnated by the divine will. The law doesn't know why it does what it does nor what it is doing, it knows only to do.

We shall never understand the Science of Mind as a science if we depend only upon the inspiration of spiritual illumination, which I value above everything else, or if we depend only on the idea that our individual thought does something somewhere. We have no individual power! There is no such thing. I have no individual mathematics. I individualize it. The moment I imagine that I have my own individual mathematics I am limited in its use to the numbers I can handle. All progress starts with thought, and we have no mind which belongs to us, but we individualize a Universal Mind.

Now the authority for spiritual mind treatment in the metaphysical field lies in the assumption that there is a mind principle, a law, which operates automatically as a mechanical, mathematical, blind force. I know there are those people who take objection to this because we all want the feeling of the Spirit and we all want to soar. We love the feeling but we must not let ourselves get drunk with it. Always, we have a principle we are going to use and apply. I can soar as high as anyone but I must, however, return to earth. So let us not just talk theories. Anyone who is familiar with the Science of Mind knows that his spiritual mind treatment is acted upon by a power greater than he is. The only authority he has to give the treatment, and to identify it with the purpose for which he gives it, is through knowing that his word becomes the law, under that principle, and does that whereunto it is spoken. Such an argument, logically presented to mind, causes the results. Unless we understand scientific methods of treatment and know that they will work, we, as individuals, shall only have results in those rare moments of inspiration, which too often are actually only moments of desperation and perspiration and nothing ever happens.

A spiritual mind practitioner is one who knows that any argument, assertion, or affirmation logically presented to mind, or inspiration so stated that there is no longer anything in his thinking except the Spirit which bears witness to the fact, is immutable law unto the thing to which the word is spoken. The word bears within itself as an entity, the intelligence, capacity and ability to fulfill itself, finding the ways, the methods, and the means for its own completion. We are speaking here of the way the microcosm works within the macrocosm, or, as Jesus said, ". . . what he (the Son) seeth the Father do: for what things soever he doeth, these also doeth the Son likewise."

Since the Universal Mind is resident everywhere, and also of necessity within us, this logical argument, assumption, or spiritual assertion is made only within ourselves. We do not "send out" anything. We do not concentrate anything, or will, or wish anything. I would like to say at this point that only those who are already familiar with this field of thought know what is implied here; and this is not said to convey any sense of superiority, for it isn't meant that way. It must be remembered, however, that this field of thought is not physiology, and it is not psychology.

We recognize and acknowledge these two fields, and we should understand and know them. For instance, it is well for us to know that at the core of every neurosis there are four elements—a sense of rejection, guilt, insecurity, or anxiety. It is well to know that the fundamental need of our emotional nature is to be wanted, needed and loved, and that the ego must not be rejected and that the mind must be forgiven. This knowledge alone, rightly handled, would probably heal half of the people who are sick. However, we desire to go beyond these fields, beyond the neurosis and the neurotic, to that which made the neurosis which made the neurotic, to that which made it possible for there to be the neurosis that made the neurotic! We shall never reach the ultimate—the Absolute, however, while we remain in any one field. There are things in *apparent* relationship to each other, which seemingly only find their causation from such relationship instead of from that to which all relationships must inevitably and eternally be relative. Troward stated it another way, saying, "We enter the Absolute to such degree as we withdraw from the relative." This is a dangerous statement because too many people do not realize that *the relative is the Absolute at the level of the relative!*

Too often metaphysicians finally reach a point where they

deny everything they do not like, and affirm everything they do like. Consider, for instance, treating for a case at law. When someone comes to me and asks, "Will you treat for my case?" I say, "No, I won't take *your* case. I will work for you and for the case, but I will not work that you will win it." The usual reply is, "Then what is the use of my asking you to work for me?" I answer, "There is no use; you are just wasting your time." When he inquires what it is we do, I tell him that I can only treat so that whatever the truth is, is made known, and that it cannot fail to be revealed. I tell him not to become angry with me, for through my work he might lose the case. I add, "If you are wrong you will lose it, because I am going to treat that there is no judge, no jury, no plaintiff, no defendant, no witness to contradict the truth or believe in anything opposite to it. I do not know what the truth is, but the Truth knows what the truth is." It is in this way that we use a power greater than ourselves. He may ask how is it that we can use a power greater than ourselves? How? We do it every time we set a hen!

A man recently said to me, "I like what you are doing but I am technically trained. I am an engineer. I can't get my intellect out of the way and yet I know I have to. Help me, won't you?"

I said, "You go home and meditate tonight and after you finish your meditation, turn to your intellect and say, 'All right, intellect, go lay an egg.' "

"Oh," he said, "don't be facetious!"

"I'm not facetious," I replied, "because if your intellect can't lay an egg, how are you ever going to get a chicken?"

How is he, or you, ever going to get a chicken? This is important to remember. The will is not creative, it is merely the point of volition. Always IT must sing, not unto us, but in us.

As Troward said, "We enter the Absolute in such degree as we withdraw from the relative," and vice versa. I don't care too much for the expression because it sounds like we start from the relative and go into the Absolute and there is no such action. As I have already said, the relative *is* the Absolute at the level of the relative, and all we mean by the relative is that there is that which has a relationship to something greater than itself. We are not talking about God *and* something. There is not God *and* something else, but only God *in* all things. "I am that I am, besides which there is none other."

If you wish to see whether or not you are "entering the Absolute," ask yourself, "in my thinking does the answer to this problem depend upon anything past, present or future?" If it does, your treatment stops at that degree of relativity which automatically makes the manifestation contingent upon the decisions already made by all parties concerned, and the whole human mind at that level of relativity. For instance, there are certain diseases which are termed incurable. If our treatment stops at the idea of the incurability of the disease, then it is incurable.

It is recognized now that alcoholism is not a disease, it is usually an escape mechanism in operation as a result of the disease. It is stated by Alcoholics Anonymous, who are the best in their field, that you can't help an alcoholic unless he wants to be helped! In our field it is often said that you can't treat someone unless he wants to be treated and then he has to give up his "sin" or his "errors." This is all nonsense! It is stopping at the level of the relativity which created the situation in the first place, which is the very condition to be changed.

If alcoholism is an escape, then its motivation is an escape.

We have to get behind the manifest physical and psychic escape, back to that which doesn't run away from anything. This hasn't anything to do with the man's opinion whatsoever. Not a thing! If it did, then our treatment would already be subject to his conscious and unconscious opinion, which is what we are treating.

The law cannot be fooled! Too many of us are running around affirming everything we would like to have, and denying everything we do not like by saying it is unreal. This is not the way the principle works. We have to get back of every effect, not only physically, but psychically and psychologically.

I understand some psychology, and a little psychiatry, probably more than most people in our field, and try to keep up to date on them. These fields, however, are merely ways to show us how to govern *our* thinking, to try to keep it the straight thinking it should be.

We believe in an absolute, unconditioned, first Cause, operating spontaneously, through self-proclamation, and answering only unto Itself out of an immutable law that is contained within Itself. Because this Mind is self-existent, self-creating, self-perpetuating, self-animating and self-expressing, it possesses everything necessary to create anything that is ever going to be, or ever was, or ever shall be. This is what we believe, and these are the two great realities with which we deal. We know that the consciousness of the Presence, the motivation of Love, and the feeling of the desire to give, which partakes of the nature of the original giving, brings back into wholeness that which seemed to be sheared off. We know that everything seeks this wholeness as the river seeks the ocean. We know this, but a scientific spiritual mind practitioner is one who, understanding it, realizes that he often has to resort to a method or a technique. This, most of us have to do most of the time!

Too many practitioners say, "I only believe in giving one treatment." I often called their bluff in past years for I used to be much meaner than I am now. I would say to them, "All right, I have a man for whom I have been working for nine months and I think he is a little worse. You just come in and speak the word!" I have never known one of them who had nerve enough to back up his claim! This is not the way the principle works. It is a false assumption, for our work is not a case of screaming and yelling, "God look at me and man look at me." Definitely not!

In the silence of your own consciousness, alone with the great Reality, you balance the account. Not in the other person's mind to see whether he should be an alcoholic or a consumptive, but in your own mind to see whether or not you have true love and givingness, and more conviction to bring to bear, not to influence the Law, but *to be operated upon by the Law* with a mathematical and mechanical certainty at the level of your conviction. If you cannot depend upon the Law with mathematical and mechanical certainty, then you have to wait for the moment of inspiration.

Emerson said, "It is easy enough in these rare moments of the silence and the solitude to maintain this terrific independence, but the great man is he who in the midst of the crowd shall keep with sweetness the independence of his solitude."

We have to depend upon the integrity of a law which reacts to us as we react to it. This is our authority. It is only because there is such a law that faith operates. In my estimation, there is no such thing as a special dispensation of providence through personal intervention.

Perhaps you read the article entitled "Master, Heal Him!" which appeared in the *Reader's Digest.* * It tells about a man who received an injury to his hip in a train wreck, and was lying unconscious in a hospital. He and his wife sang in a church choir each Sunday and she was to have sung a solo on this particular Sunday. The man wasn't expected to live and the doctors did not dare operate. The minister told the congregation, "I know that she would like us to pray for him. Now, first," he said, "direct your faith and your love," which is the conviction and feeling, for God speaks to the heart. He may have asked them to get down on their knees, I don't know and who cares? That has nothing to do with it. Then the minister turned to the great Healer and prayed, to Jesus I have no doubt.

But suppose the minister had been a Mohammedan, then to whom would he have prayed? To whom would a Buddhist or a Hindu have prayed? Let us not think because we proudly claim to be Christians that God speaks only to the Christian! Remember, Jesus had never heard of a Christian! Emerson said, "For every stoic there is a stoic, but in Christendom where is the Christian?" The Christian is one who gives up his life to find it and doesn't care what the cost is. He is one who desires everyone's good equal with his own. He is one who has such confidence in God that he isn't afraid of anything. He is one who has such humility that he has no pride. He is one who is so simple that he can never be arrogant, and he is one who stands aside even when the great or the near great are screaming, and doesn't hear their noise. It is a very difficult thing to be a Christian!

Well, we don't care to whom the minister and his congregation prayed. I always say, "I thank the God that is, that the

*August, 1953

God that is believed in, isn't!'' I believe that the God that is, responds to each one of us in the form, the method, and the manner of the God that is believed in; that is why Jesus said it is done unto you as you believe.

No doubt the minister got down on his knees, and prayed to his saviour, saying, in effect, ''There is a fellow over here in a certain hospital and you are going to go with us. This is the street and here is the hospital and we are going to enter it, and here in a certain corridor is the door to his room. Now, we are going to open the door. There is the fellow over there in bed, and there is something wrong with him and we ask that you go over and lay your hand on his head.'' Is there anything more specific and direct than that? Not that the prayer has to be so specific, but the thing that struck me in this story is the very definiteness of the prayer. I am sure that the minister knew why he was praying the way he did. He was tracing out the steps for the congregation. Sometimes we must do that, but we must always know that the law is impersonal and that it is creative, if we are going to use a principle and not just try to become inspired. I believe in both, of course, but we have to combine them. The Spirit and the Letter, the Bible terms them, and one is the complement of the other. One is the feeling, the other is the mold or the manner in which the feeling is expressed.

In our conviction we must combine a realization with a knowledge and acceptance. We must have a conviction that is no longer refuted in our own mind. At the level of our spiritual awareness there must be no question that an action will take place which will manifest that spiritual awareness for and through the person or thing with which we have identified our thought, prayer or treatment. Therefore, if we are going to teach a method, we must teach the steps of it, and the way it works. There is no other way. We may call it affirmation and denial, or we may call it an argument. It doesn't matter what we call it, but it must be taught.

In every school of metaphysics the whole system of spiritual mind treatment is invariably based on Quimby's concept that "mind is matter in solution and matter is mind in form," but that the matter in solution and the mind in form is the dual nature of that which he termed "a superior wisdom." The "Quimby Manuscripts" is one of the most original books in the world. Our whole system of teaching is based upon Quimby's concept that the things which have to be resolved are mental, not physical. We must be able to reduce everything to mind, or consciousness, because consciousness does not operate upon something external to itself. Consciousness *is* the one great reality in the universe. In other words, our thought does not spiritualize matter and it does not materialize Spirit. Spirit and matter, or thought and form, are one and the same thing.

Modern physics deals with matter and energy but not with matter as separate from energy. The physicist does not deny the reality of the objective experience but he does deny, however, that the causation is separate from the intelligence which originated it. We do not say that people are not sick, poor, weak and unhappy. We do say it is not necessary to experience these illnesses.

We must have a *feeling of authority in the power of our word,* but, like the authority and power in any law in nature, *it has to be impersonal.* We don't put the power in our word, we take it out. We don't put anything in anything! As I pursue a line of thought through, I ask myself, "To what conclusion does this lead me?" We have to maintain the independence and the integrity of our own individuality, or we shall be lost, and we are not supposed to be lost, but

found. In other words, we must not be superstitious. Sometimes I wish I might be, and yet I know that superstition is a
form of regression. The kind of thinking of the poet who
said, "Turn backward, O time, in thy flight, make me a child
again just for tonight," is psychological regression. It is
beautiful, and I can cry while I say it—I feel so sorry for
myself! I admit that I often use such quotations, for if people
are going to cry, they might as well cry over something beautiful. It is well for us to cry, but we must laugh, too. Such
statements stem from a sense of morbidity unredeemed in
our own minds. We are still thinking of the old guy with
whiskers, believing we are condemned; but now that we are
"saved" we are not going anywhere where the weather is very
dry to say the least!

We want to escape both superstition and regression if we
can. However, in making the escape through the authority of
the law we must be careful to avoid that very peculiar thing
which can happen to metaphysicians if they think that God is
only a principle. We may exercise the right of authority to the
impersonal law *only* as we have communed with the personalness of the Spirit. I have no superstitions and I have consider-
able ability to abstract my thought, but I doubt if anyone
believes more in the intimacy of communion with the Divine
Spirit, which must be personal to me in a unique way, for the
same reason that my thumbprint is different from yours.
There must be something which I can do, which nobody ever
did before, and never will be done again. Emerson said that
imitation is suicide. We find we deal with an impersonal law,
and just because we have a sensing of the personalness of
Spirit—the glory and the beauty of it—do not think the Law
isn't in operation! It is at this point, however, subject to the
Spirit.

Another principle we must know, use, and must come to understand, is that a treatment rightfully given is absolutely independent of every theory of physical cause and effect, of psychic cause and effect, or psychosomatic relationships. The Law is aware only in a mechanical way. It knows what it is doing but it doesn't know it is doing what it is doing, nor why. Electricity doesn't know that it produces light. When you plant a potato should the potato know it is a potato, it might protest, and say that it wanted to be something else. The potato, however, cannot be something else. The Law always functions this way.

We have the privilege of personal communion with Spirit and the authority to use the Law, but the assumption is not ours personally. We use the Law much in the same manner as we would when we throw a rock off the cliff. Will it or will it not strike the bottom? It will unless something interferes with it. We must have assurance in our authority to use the Law, but not by the arrogance of putting on a peculiar look and thinking we must be spiritual geniuses. Maybe we are, I don't know. I hope we are, but we must always know that the Law is the servant of the Spirit, as we learn to know how it works, and we must never be talked out of that knowledge by any living soul.

We believe that for every visible object there is a divine pattern of that object in the invisible to which the object is related. This applies to a bed, the grass, or an archangel, if such a creature exists and I suppose he does! There must be beings beyond us as we are beyond tadpoles, but it will be time enough to consider this when we arrive at that next state of consciousness. We really wouldn't know how to be an archangel right now! I can conceive in my imagination a beauty so splendid that should I perceive it now it would shatter even my physical being. There must be such beauty because now we do see only in part and beyond that which we do see is more and more. Always there is something locked behind the border, something yet to learn. We always find it so, and the search and seeking is eternal. The Spirit will be true to Itself at every level of expression but It will never be completed. If It were ever to be completed, then we should have to add the assumption of completion, continuation and eternal boredom, and then even God would become tired of Himself! God is doing something to and through every one of us all the time. As Emerson said, "the ancient of days is in the latest invention."

We must have the assumption of law and order, as well as Presence and Spirit, but it must be the assumption of an impersonal law in operation, an impersonal principle which the individual uses. It is only then that we can make the complete surrender because we know in what we believe as well as in whom we believe.

The one who practices the science of spiritual mind treatment is one who is ever more seeking to partake of the Spirit. He believes in this above all else. To him God has become the one great and final Reality, not to the loss of anything else, but to the discovery that we are all found in God. As to techniques for effective prayer, Jesus said, "Heaven and earth shall pass away, but my words shall not pass away." When Isaiah was asked the meaning of the story of the sowers, he said, "So shall my word be the law; this is the law, this is the prophets."

The seed is the *word*. We must know that our word, being the presence and the power and the activity of the Spirit in us *is* the law of elimination unto that which does not belong in our experience. But we do not put the power into the Law that makes our word become manifest! If we did, we wouldn't know how, and if we knew how and had to do it, it would be very exhausting. A spiritual treatment that tires one is a bad treatment. A treatment in which we use "will" is a bad treatment. A treatment that "sends" anything out is a bad treatment. A treatment that limits itself to any existing circumstance is a bad treatment. When I say it is a bad treatment I mean that it isn't effective, that it isn't what it should be.

In sensing the Presence and understanding the Law, there can be a complete abandonment of the intellect and the will. However, I think that even in such abandonment there must be the formation of some kind of a pattern, for while I believe that every object in this world is related to its divine pattern, I also believe that divine patterns are eternally being made. When you design a new dress you don't think that the dress has ever been made before, do you? Every day a new song is sung! I think that God composes all the music, and sings all the songs, but He is singing them in every singer, right now, and he doesn't have to repeat Himself, for there is no monotony in the divine Life. It is always creating a fresh and unique variation of Itself, and so I believe that as we come to sense the divine Presence, the Father, the Spirit, the something that we feel and which certainly can't be put into words, there is a great and abiding emotional feeling of Reality.

There is nothing in this feeling that will ever make us peculiar. Nothing! During the greatest spiritual experiences that I have ever had, and they are experiences that we do not talk about, I was *more* myself and not less. There was no loss of my identity but an accentuation of it. The feeling is never one of absorption, it is always a sense of immersion. You have a greater realization than you ever had before as to who you are.

I repeat that it is very difficult to get rid of superstition in our field. We must learn that there is no saviour but ourselves! There is no mediator but Christ in you—"the hope of glory." There is nothing between It and us; God comes fresh and new and clean as Presence, and the universe presents itself as principle. By putting the two together we shall glorify "the fire from Heaven" as inspiration and illumination.

I believe in what Emerson called "the lonely listener," but when we use the Law we use it as a definite principle; it acts according to definite rules and performs in a certain way. There is no caprice in it, for it is inevitable; it is immutable. It is certain to act. If we know this when we are treating and do not seem to get results, we return to Spirit and say, "There is just a little more work to be done within myself, not out 'there.' " There is nothing out "there." The causation is inside and so we work until we see the thing clearly. What do we do? We meet the great Reality as Presence and Law, and we are confronted with what all the great and wise have believed in—the divine ideas and eternal patterns of Life.

I do not believe that evil or disease belong to anyone, or that they should be located in anyone. Our task is to separate the belief from the believer. In psychology they say the neurosis must be separated from the neurotic. Have we enough spiritual awareness so that the reaction of the Law of the Word, which is immutable, will cover the lack of faith, the lack of love, or whatever it is that seems to be needed? Are we able to forgive deeply enough, to love greatly enough, to feel broadly enough? Is there enough beauty in our souls to paint the picture, or sing the song for someone else in our own hearts? If there is, we shall see it made manifest.

You must be able to meet the great Reality alone, without fear, simply, joyfully and easily in a relaxed mental way, and at the same time must rely upon the integrity of the Law. Who was so simple and humble as Einstein? Who was more simple than Jesus? A man who isn't like this cannot do it! Jesus understood what we are talking about. Einstein knows mathematics. They know *IT!* They know that heaven and earth shall pass away but that the WORD will not pass away. *That is our authority!*

Unless we can conceive of such a principle, our work will not be good. We cannot think of the results of spiritual mind treatment as depending upon the caprice of the divine will or on our own whimsical fancy. Today, if I feel right, I may catch some inspiration, and if I feel right tomorrow I will write a little more of the story, or sing a little more of the song, or give a treatment. The author, painter, or technician cannot work this way, and neither can you. You must sit down and do your work consciously and solicitously and say, "Here I am and I can do it now."

The Law must be so real to you that you know that you trust yourself, because you trust it! This is spiritual mind practice, and it is not well enough understood. The simplest explanation you can give anyone so that they may understand it, is to say: There is a mind principle which acts upon an argument logically presented to it, which will produce a result commensurate with the realization at the center of the mind of the one who makes the argument. The argument is spontaneous, the reaction is mechanical; nothing can stop the principle from working. If, on the other hand, you do not want to think about the Law and want only to think of the Spirit, you will have to use inspiration and say: The Spirit bears witness to the inspiration and the witness is the effect. We all believe this but it would be better for us, and for the whole world, if we would combine the two, since they are the two parts of the one nature.

I believe that we have the clearest teaching the world has ever known. The more experience and understanding we gain, the greater are the values gained, and we come at last to know that we have neither God nor man to prove anything to, only to ourselves. We come, too, to know that we dare not refuse ourselves the gratification of that knowledge, the authority of that Law, and the feeling of that Presence—the beauty of that ineffable something which is indescribable, but which we all know and feel; that something which through the Law of Its own Word spoke the world into being!

Let us commune with that Presence, and use that Power, in the beauty and quiet of this moment.

Indraw and breathe into us, O Eternal Spirit, everything that stands for beauty, everything that is meant by power, and law and order, warmth and color, the artistry of life and the certainty of love and friendship; impregnate our souls now with Thy Spirit. Amen.

"Infinite Spirit, Thou who lights the morning star,
   Uplift our souls to Thine embrace.
May we reach out and in all creation see Thy face;
See Thee even in the first faint cry of the
   babe at the mother's breast.
See Thee when the noon is high, and when all
   nature sinks to rest;
On bed of pain, on bed of ease, we feel Thy
   Presence in the night,
At break of dawn when we awake, we see Thee in
   the morning light."

(Author unknown)

May our minds be so open to the Infinite abundance of love and beauty, compassion and goodness, simplicity and sincerity, that it flows around the world bringing back, as it must, the joy that is God. Amen.

E. H.

CHAPTER FIVE

Making Life A Success

The perception or realization of abundance is the background for the consciousness of supply!

We strain too much to make our demonstrations. A demonstration is nothing less than the simple fact that through some action in your own mind upon the Cosmos, which provides the inevitable necessity of a different reaction from the Cosmos and the Law of Mind in action, ideas are brought into play and made manifest in our experience that were not there before, or made better than they were before. This is done without helping or pushing the ideas along. This is the way a demonstration is made, and is the only way we can know that we have made one.

When I first started this movement, I thought that I knew this principle. Now I know that I only know about half of it. At that time, however, I thought I knew it all and that I could teach the world. I sat in my office for six months and only one person came to see me and he thought I was insane! At the end of the six months I was like the old prophet with long whiskers. Someone had told him that anyone who wore long whiskers was a fool. So when he went home he lit a candle, because it was dark, to look into the mirror to see if he looked like a fool. The candle flame ignited his whiskers and the result was a burned face, and he said, ''Verily, anyone who wears long whiskers is a fool!'' He demonstrated it!

That six-month period was a very disconcerting experience,

because it threw me completely off the track. I did have sense enough to realize that what I believed was true but I didn't understand it well enough. I said to myself, "It has to be true. The mathematics of this principle is right; its inspiration is right. The great, the good, and the wise have believed in it, and it is the foundation for all the modern metaphysical movements. There is something wrong and it has to be with me." So I closed the office, sold the furniture, and secured a position as purchasing agent with the city. I said to myself, however, "I am going to teach this principle and I am going to teach it to the multitudes, but I will never cross this room to initiate a movement for it because this time it is going to work through me. How else will I know?"

I held to that decision and nothing happened for many months. One day when the superintendent of streets was in my office, he asked, "What is this book that you are reading, Ernest? It looks good to me." He had picked up one of Troward's books off my desk and was looking at it.

I said, "Take it with you. You are an engineer and the man who wrote this book was a scientific man, too. He was also a judge, a very intelligent man, and you will understand him."

He read it and later asked me, "Why couldn't I invite a few friends into my home and you talk to them about this?"

He did, and about the third time we met together one of the women said to me, "I did a crazy thing today. I was up town and I made arrangements for you to speak in a certain hall next week." Within two years from that time, without putting an announcement in the newspapers, I was speaking to between twenty-five hundred and three thousand people a week.

At about that time I experienced another difficulty which I had to work out. I had a large practice but I found that almost no one paid me. Now let all practitioners and leaders listen. I had very little income. I could pay my rent and I was still eating but I was no longer receiving a pay check every two weeks from the city, for I had quit that job. So I treated everyone I could think of and everything I saw—the woods, the flowers, and so on, and then one day in my office I sat down in my chair and said, "I'll never get up from this chair until I know why people do not pay me!" Because I had made a *definite* assertion, I had no sooner said it when I stood right up and exclaimed, "Why, I don't expect them to!" I wanted them to pay me but I hadn't expected them to do so.

Troward said that a neurotic thought pattern, which is morbid, repeats itself with monotonous regularity throughout life until it is changed, and that was a kind of morbid thought pattern. Then I realized that I had to treat *myself* because the thought pattern had nothing to do with my clients. It couldn't, for I wasn't letting them pay me. They did want to pay me because after I had gotten my thinking straight about it, within thirty days many people I had worked for came in and paid me, saying that they had just forgotten to do so. There is nothing to treat but your own thought!

I had another experience which taught me a great deal about the consciousness of supply. In the earlier days of our work one of the loveliest practitioners we have ever had on our staff took an office next to mine; this was before we had our own building. About a year later she told me that she would have to give up her office, and when I asked her why, she said she was not making enough to pay the rent and could not keep it. I said to her, "Why I thought you had a large practice."

She replied, "Oh, I am busy every minute."

"Oh," I said, "that's ridiculous. You should be making

very good money. You know there is nothing wrong in being paid for your work.''

Although I know there are people who think that you shouldn't be paid for spiritual mind treatment, I do not believe that there is anything wrong in being paid for the work that we do. I would suggest that these people examine their thinking, examine the underlying motive of this belief. They might be surprised as to what they will find!

This practitioner was a sweet and sincere person. She was what I call the ''religious'' type, much more religious than I am! I questioned her about her background and it developed that all her life she had worked for social welfare organizations, either for the county or state, the city, or church. Immediately I saw the cause of her problem. She had always expected to give but had never expected to be given to! When she asked me what she could do about it, I said, ''That's easy. We will just reverse the thought pattern.'' Within a few months she became one of the most successful practitioners we have ever had.

I have noticed, too, that those practitioners who come from a certain social background will draw to them, automatically, the people from that background as clients. The Law works that way. For many years a certain man on our staff sold real estate for the large Pandora Company of California. Now almost his entire practice is with big business people, not small ones. Not that it makes any difference whether they are big or little business people, but this is the way our consciousness reflects and expresses.

We can, if we are not careful, get caught in what I call a ''cosmic trap,'' which I do not think is of our own making but comes from the race consciousness. It is the belief that in order to be good you must suffer, and to be in religion you must take the blows of adversity. There is nothing in our philosophy to cause us to want to be a doormat or a book-mark! We do not wish to be arrogant, either. We must have the capacity to love greatly, but justice and mercy must balance. The universe is just without judgment. It is also giving. Never let someone else decide what is right or wrong for you, because they do not know. Ask yourself if the desire or idea you have complies with the Law of Truth, of righteousness. Does it partake of the nature of Reality? If it does, then you can go the limit with it.

Every practitioner and leader in our field should be success-ful. Everyone in our field should be successful. The old mor-bid concept of suffering for righteousness' sake comes up too often in our work. You will hear someone say, ''This is being given to me to see how much I can take!'' That is all nonsense and we should not say such things nor believe them. Such a statement is said in ignorance of the Law, which excuses no one from its effects. It is going right back to the concept of the old man in the sky with the long whiskers, and he isn't there!

> The little man upon the stair
> and again he wasn't there;
> He wasn't there again today;
> Oh, God, I wish he'd go away!

A friend of mine wrote another verse to that poem—

> The little man upon the stair,
> Who was so consistently not there;
> The only thing I have to say,
> I think he must have come to stay!

Nothing could sound sillier and yet it was written by one of the most brilliant men we have had in our movement.

As long as you have the doormat attitude, that will be your

judge. Be careful of the things you think and say. Remember that arrogance, too, is false.

Another false idea that crops up in the metaphysical field is the tendency among people to advertise, blazingly, how to get rich. We have no formulae for getting rich.

A man said to me one day, "I want to have a million dollars; will you please treat that I know how to get it?"

I asked him about how long he thought it would take. He wasn't sure. Then I asked him, "About how much do you think I will receive?"

"Well," he said, "you will probably get at least a thousand dollars, and I will pay you."

Then I asked him, "Don't you suppose that I might keep the million and give you the thousand?"

Such thinking doesn't make sense. I shudder when I see signs which say "think and grow rich," and yet there is a certain amount of truth in it when we have the consciousness of abundance.

The practitioner or leader in our field who has the consciousness of poise and balance should treat himself, not the patient who tries to "use" him. The patient will then change his attitude or he will leave so that there will be in the practitioner's environment only what should be there and which he has the right to have. If the practitioner refuses to accept his own divine birthright, he is foolish.

I make no hesitation in saying we are here to serve the Truth and not to be used by any living soul. There should be no arrogance in us about this, for we must work with our people and we should work with them more and more. However, if we are not successful, and I believe we are all successful, or that each draws to himself that which is like himself through the immutable Law of cause and effect, let us not feel that

God is trying us and that we ought to suffer a little because it shows how much we can take "for God's sake."

Emerson said, "The ancient of days is in the latest invention." We know that the principle itself is such that if a man wants to invent a machine that would drill a hole through spaghetti, and if he correctly applies the principle, he will invent one. It will happen even though the man has never heard of a spaghetti machine before. The very idea that makes the demand answers in the terms of the demand that is made. This is the way the principle works for us.

In all the philosophic thinking of today this principle is recognized and is called "the emergent evolution." It means that the principle of nature answers the demand nature makes upon the principle in the terms of the demand made. When we needed fingernails, we got them; when we needed toes, they developed. We are all unconsciously making demands upon life all the time.

If I jump up and scream, "I am rich; all that God has is mine," that is dynamic, but unless it means something to me, unless I am One with the substance of the belief, nothing will happen. We find, however, that we can change the neurotic thought patterns that repeat themselves. Zoroaster said that there is an inertia in thought patterns which seems to resist even argument and you would think that discarnate spirits were talking, but they are not. The "things" which talked back to Jesus and said their "name was legion" was the multiple personality of the instrument through which it spoke. It said, in effect, "Bring on your gang; where are the rest of the disciples? I am ready to fight."

This reminds me of a story about a Hollywood producer. The studio was filming a picture about Jesus, and the producer came into the studio one day and saw twelve men standing around and asked his assistant who they were. He was told they were the disciples. Did Jesus have disciples, he asked? How many? Twelve was the answer and here they are. He said, "Twelve disciples! Haven't I told you over and over again that this is going to be a production? Go out and hire at least a hundred!"

These thought patterns do repeat themselves monotonously, not only the ones that give us neuroses, but the ones that keep us poor. There is only one Principle of Mind in operation and we are dealing with this same principle whether it is in the melancholy attitude of a neurotic morbid fear, or in the ecstasy of the mystics. There are not many principles—one for you and one for me, one for someone who has red hair and one for someone who is bald. There is just *one* Principle and it reacts to us at different levels.

For instance, there is the person who is filled with a sense of self-isolation, a feeling that no one loves him. Now I have told you that our first emotional need is to be wanted, needed and loved; that the libido must have an object, and the ego must not be rejected. If it is, and this monotonous thought pattern of isolation remains unhealed, it acts like a searchlight. It attracts fear and says, "I don't like that person and he doesn't like me; I don't get along with him." Then when this object is taken away, his searchlight throws out a beam and attracts another person of the same kind. There is only one neurosis and only one form of the neurosis and it projects itself everywhere, making it appear as though what is inside is outside. If what is on the inside is changed, however, what is outside will change or disappear.

In changing the thought patterns through spiritual mind treatment, let us be careful how we use the principle. Dynamic treatment must be very ego satisfying! I noticed with what dynamic power I walked down from the cabin this morning. With every step I took I said, "Gravitational force, *hold* me in place!" And it did! These dynamic treatments aren't worth writing home about, for as Shakespeare said, "Thou dost protest too loudly." I think that through his poetic insight he had a glimpse of that muse which Emerson said, "Sits astride our neck and writes through our hand." It overpowers our intellect and causes the feeling to become the obedient servant of the Spirit which is beyond and greater than ourselves. Every great writer must feel it or he would never enter into greatness.

Let me repeat that there is only *one* Law of Mind in action. There is only *one* Spirit, and at the different levels of our perception of Spirit, the Law reacts. We can just as well create a thought pattern of abundance as one of lack. I do not have a million dollars and I do not feel that I need them, but I certainly see to it that I am supplied with what I do need. I am more interested in love and friendship than I am in money, although I believe they are both mine. I would suspect myself if people didn't like me and I would treat myself to know how much I love people. Sometimes it is difficult to do because we all have, more or less, a sense of rejection.

I know many very rich people and I can think of only two who are really happy in their wealth. They are women and they give so much. One of them gave a college five million dollars.

We are not talking about money when we talk about success. We are not talking about fame when we talk about success. Money and fame are the by-products of success. There is the fable of the ancient king who told one of his couriers to go through the countryside and find the man in his realm who was happy, and "send his shirt to me, for I want to wear it."

His agent was gone for many years and then returned one day without the shirt.

He said, "Sire, I found only one man who was happy. He was sitting at the side of the road and he just laughed all the time because he was so happy. I sat with him and laughed too. He was wonderful but he wasn't a fool."

The king asked, "Did you bring me his shirt?"

And the emissary replied, "Sire, he had none."

Maybe that is why he was happy! Wealth isn't having possessions, although there is nothing wrong with having them if you know what they mean.

The consciousness of abundance is the consciousness of life, of love, of living and giving, of the capacity to be happy, and I believe it should include whatever we need, or that which we call money because it is the medium of exchange. We can develop a consciousness of abundance if we align our thought with the bigness of life. How big is everything? Browning said, "How good is man's life, the mere living; how fit to employ all the heart and the soul and the senses forever in joy." The one who enters into love and joy, into the abundant and successful life, is the one who isn't afraid of anything. "There is nothing bad that can happen to a good man," said Socrates.

I often think of Jesus multiplying the loaves and fishes. He knew the doctrine of the Law, and present in the crowd were all the wise men who had all the answers but didn't know what they meant. Out of the vast throng of people he had to call on a little boy who didn't know that the miracle couldn't take place. I can imagine that little boy strutting up with enthusiasm to Jesus and then, jumping up and down, saying, "Here, I caught a little fish and here is a hunk of bread." You see, he didn't deny anything. Here we have the Lord of experience, the man of wisdom, and he had the help of the boy who didn't know it couldn't be done, and the miracle was performed.

Somehow or other it seems we have to get back of all the sad experience. Have we been robbed of love, of friendship, of money? Have we been robbed of substance? Have we lost everything that we had? If we have, then at long last we are now ready to turn to that foundation which knows no loss. I am not referring to the concept that we must suffer. I do not wish to suffer and I do not intend to do so any more than I can avoid. I certainly expect to make every provision I can to provide for myself and family, to live in abundance while we are in this world. I have never known anyone, however, who was ever able to take his worldly goods with him when he left this world!

How much can we give? That much will we have. It comes right back to this—how much can we love, that much affection shall be ours. To what degree can we abandon ourselves to Life, not in a silly sentimental, emotional way, which is a make-believe and a camouflage for an inferiority complex, but in the nobility of that Spirit which must offer Itself to Itself, that It may know and enjoy Itself, and put our feet out into a feeling void and find ourselves on solid rock. I know of no other success. The Word was *with* God and the Word *is* God and there is no difference. This is the consciousness of our supply!

We recognize the perfect beauty, radiance and love of the Divine Intelligence, the "Prince of Peace," complete and whole within our consciousness. Our understanding is deep and pure, and we perceive that we are ONE with all that is, and all that is, is good! And so it is.

Lord of Creation, we turn to Thee in humble gratefulness for the Divine inspiration and illumination given us. May the light of Thy countenance shine upon us evermore. Amen.

G.M.

CHAPTER SIX

Mind in Action

ur way of thinking is neither authoritative nor dog-matic, nor is it of one book, author or teacher. Rather, we believe in the enlightened thought of the world; in the intuitive revelation and scientific discovery, which are the only ways man can gain knowledge, I presume. Intuition would include religion, not theology, and I believe it would include the only true revelation there is, which is revelation through intuition. There is no God who singles out some one individual for special revelation any more than there is the possibility of an intercession to God. We cannot *persuade* God to do something for us.

We have a *science,* which is built on facts, laws, causes, and principles applicable universally; and a *philosophy,* which is our individual belief and opinion about life. Philosophy is anyone's opinion about anything. There are political, eco-nomic, spiritual, cultural and artistic philosophies, but they are just opinions. To say that philosophy means Kant and Berkeley, Jung and Emerson, is not so at all. They were merely the people who were not afraid to say what they thought and had it recorded. Philosophy can be your opinion about the weather—do you like it or don't you like it?

Now there are people who believe in the special dispensa-tion of providence but there is no such thing. There is, how-ever, a specialized one. There are those people, too, who believe there is a power which reacts to them because we intercede and ask it to. Never is this true in such degree as we believe it does so *because we* ask it to provide a way, consciously or unconsciously. If this were so, we would have a Universe whose Law is a caprice and whose intelligence is a whimsical fancy. In other words, we would have a chaos and not a cosmos. Since the Universe is a cosmos and not a chaos, this isn't the way the Law works. We recognize these truths and so we believe philosophically, intuitively, and spiritually in such revelation as we have access to which is valid and does not contradict itself. It seems that most of it does, however.

We believe that the great intuitions of the ages have always been direct perceptions of Truth; therefore, direct impartations and proclamations of the One Mind through the individual who perceives them. We have reason to believe this because every modern discovery tends to prove and demonstrate this assumption rather than to disprove it. The ancients understood the nature of the physical world, the universe, as motion and number and this is now the very last word in modern science. They also understood that everything is governed by law but that law, itself, is the servant of the Spirit, and of our own minds to such degree as we unify with the Spirit. This is now becoming understood by many of the great scientific minds of the world.

We perceive, therefore, the swingback of the cycle of intuitive perception even though it may have been intercepted during the intervening years by the belief in psychic hallucination. This belief in psychic hallucination is the unconscious projection of our own desire to declare God to be what we want God to be! This is one of the greatest fallacies of mind, and none of us are immune to this belief. We are human beings and none of us are as smart as we think we are!

However, we are struggling along doing the best we can, holding each other's hands, loving each other, and going on to greater understanding.

I believe that the intuition of the ages, if we can separate it from the psychic hallucinations, will not only tell us about the nature of Reality but will be prophetic on a spiritual plane of what is going to happen as the result of scientific discoveries. Let me differentiate between that and a psychic experience.

Two years before the atom bomb fell in Japan, at about the time they were experimenting with it down in New Mexico, I was giving a treatment one day. In the middle of the treatment I seemed to be sitting on the side of a hill overlooking a town. All at once there was an explosion. I saw a cloud rise and mushroom high in the sky exactly as it did later when the A-Bomb fell on Hiroshima, and I looked down at the town and said to myself, ''This isn't destruction, this is annihilation!'' Part of London had just been destroyed but I realized this that I saw wasn't like that kind of destruction, because the city was there and then in the next instant was gone. I knew this was going to take place and end the war. I didn't know where or when but I knew it was going to annihilate a city. So I recorded this experience and explained it to five people, who witnessed the manuscript by signature, and then I put it safely away.

Now this incident is an example of a psychic experience. It was psychic because the causation of that bombing had already been set in motion, which, mathematically, had to produce the exact result that took place unless it was intercepted. There was nothing fatalistic about it. Karma is not fate; Karma is not Kismet; it is the law of cause and effect. It could have been that those scientists, after they had seen what this energy could do, would have shuddered and said, "We will not use it." Then the causation would have been intercepted and a city would not have been destroyed. Was what happened good or bad? I do not know. We are not discussing moral issues here.

Chains of causation can be set in motion, individually or collectively, which produce their inevitable results unless they are changed. *They can be changed.*

Let me repeat that ours is not an authoritative religion. We have a textbook which is the accumulation of the greatest teachings of the ages but we haven't any idea of becoming a closed system. We have two possibilities; we can be so narrow that we never grow or we can be so broad that we have no depth. It is up to us to find the place in between which gives freedom without giving the freedom to destroy the freedom which makes the freedom possible! In the name of liberty, for instance, communism destroys freedom and this is the kind of fallacy about which I speak. We do not wish to be that way.

If I believed I had a "revelation," I would shudder at the thought, for there is no man so hypnotized as the man who coerces himself. I have often wondered if it is possible to avoid this mesmeric state. If any group ever avoids it, we will, but in order to do so we have to keep our minds open at the top for a new influx of wisdom, and we have to set up a sign which says "stop, look and listen; does this that I believe measure up to Truth?" for there are certain inevitabilities that the ages have declared to be true.

Now, let us consider the scientific aspect of our work. Einstein said he does much of his work by intuition, and Charles Kettering, one of the world's greatest engineers, said that every invention is an intuition, and that the processes of working out the techniques of the invention are a series of intuitions. Henry Ford believed that we are surrounded by a field of universal ideas from which we choose. Arthur Compton, the Nobel prize winner in physics, said that modern science has found nothing in its research which denies the general theory of a Universal Creative Mind of which we are the offspring and It is as our parent. Sir James Jeans said that we can think of the universe in terms of an infinite Thinker thinking mathematically, and Sir Arthur Eddington said that everything looks as though the universe were intelligence and the movement of the intelligence is its mathematics and its law. Dr. Alexis Carrel said that faith works like a law.

Yes, our work is scientific. All that any science is is that some person, or group of people, who, believing in a certain principle and that it must work in a certain way, act as though it were so and subject themselves to experiments of trial and error to determine the validity of the principle. If it does work, they give this knowledge to other people and the principle works just as correctly for them when they subject themselves to it. The principle that is established does not belong to those who discover it or use it.

We have such a science. It is the Law of Mind in Action; it is Mind Itself ready to act. This is the principle. We have a religion, too, which is the belief in a Divine Presence back of the principle.

Probably two of the greatest spiritualistic mediums who ever lived were Arthur Ford and Eileen Garrett. Now what will happen to their spiritualistic hypothesis when Dr. Rhine in his scientific research at Duke University, or someone else, shall have finally developed people who do not have to use that hypothesis but will reproduce everything that is now produced in a spiritualistic seance? There isn't any question about this for they are already doing it at Duke University. What will happen is what ought to happen, and that is that you and I should know that we are as spiritual now as we are ever going to become!

Scientific research is not new to us. About ten years ago I organized a group of fifty people for such a purpose, some of whom are still working with me, who really know their metaphysical onions, so to speak, and know how to apply them. At that time a woman friend of mine was supervisor of the insane hospitals in this state. I went to her and asked her to pick at random ten patients from each of the four mental hospitals for whom we would do treatment work. I told her that we didn't care who they were, what their backgrounds were, nor what the physical diagnoses were. I asked her to send us reports from time to time concerning the progress of these patients. None of the patients or hospital personnel knew we were doing the work. We worked for two years and the number of these people discharged from the hospitals was very high in ratio compared to those who were discharged for other reasons.

Later, we conducted the same experiment for some three hundred alcoholics. We discovered that it made no difference whether these patients knew they were being treated or not. If it made any difference as to whether they wanted to be treated or not, I couldn't say. We must stick to the Truth so closely, so tightly, that we even walk backwards for fear we will overestimate our concepts, because the one thing we should never do, individually or collectively, is to get an individual or collective bighead. It might explode some day, for it only takes so much pressure! The results with the alcoholics were a little better than eighty-five percent, and it didn't make any difference whether they knew they were being treated or not.

You might ask me if we have the right to treat someone without their consent and I would ask you, in return, what do you think treatment is? Do you think it is mental coercion? Our work is *not* mental coercion. If you went out on the street and found a man run over by a car, unconscious, and with his legs broken, would you have the right to call an ambulance? You wouldn't have any right not to call it. Remember, in such degree as anything is wrong with us from the standpoint of a higher sanity, we are mentally unbalanced, for these ills do not belong to the nature of the Divinity that is within us. Of course we have the right to treat the other fellow without his knowledge that we are doing so. To think otherwise is just another superstition.

We know we have accumulated the best "stuff" up to the present time but we do not think the last word has been said. We want what the rest of the world has to offer and we are willing to accept it, for we learn from all of the sciences. We have learned from psychology that an emotional bias will create an intellectual blind spot. Therefore, we know that a person whose sole bias is that he alone knows the Truth will not find any more Truth because there is nobody at home to accept it! We know that where there is an inhibition in the psyche of a practicing psychologist, he cannot see straight for the patient and the analysis stops. If the blind lead the blind, they will both fall into the ditch. We know that love is superior to hate, as Dr. Menninger tells us. We are continuing to learn, and we should be extremely intelligent in our work.

Probably in our field of thought more than in any other field, for instance, we are apt to become confused over the two entirely different ideas of psychic hallucination and spiritual illumination.

I have watched Dr. Hammond and Dr. Hill perform. They

were two of the most outstanding authentic scientific investigators in the field of psychic phenomena. During seances, which they conducted, I witnessed nineteen materializations as solid as my body, which apparently had flesh and blood and circulatory systems. We could weigh them, shake hands with them, and talk with them. They wore clothes and were *apparently* real, but of course I do not believe they were real at all! They were real as phenomena, yes. There was no doubt about that, for no chicanery was performed, and these materializations were not illusions. An illusion cannot be produced, as a manifestation, that has weight, substance and a voice, whose heartbeats can be measured, unless there is some form of circulation.

I have also seen the precipitation of the most beautiful pictures imaginable—landscapes, seascapes, and perfect portraits of people in color.

There is no man living who knew more about such phenomena than Hamlin Garland. He wrote the book "Forty Years in Psychic Research." One time when I visited him he was developing a medium. When I say he was developing a medium, I do not mean that he was a spiritualist. He was merely developing someone who had mediumistic powers, and by the word "mediumistic," I mean psychic. This person would stand on an ordinary scratchpad and writing would come through the paper. Once a certain drawing was precipitated on a slate and Garland couldn't tell whether the substance used was chalk or crayon. So he sent a sample of it to a laboratory to be tested and they wrote back that it was impossible to analyze for it was an unknown substance.

I have heard beautiful music, and once I heard a whole mass in Latin. One other time, just after Valentino and Jack Pickford had died, we asked, through this medium, for Jack to appear. All of us present had known him. We asked him, when he apparently appeared, what he was doing and he said he was writing a play with Valentino!

Any person who knows anything about such phenomena will not deny their existence. The person who denies them is ignorant of their significance. The phenomena do exist. I have seen things come through solid walls that you could take home and keep. One group which investigates these forces, as they are called, has a whole museum of such phenomena.

Now I am not attempting to persuade any of you to believe in such phenomena. If you were to read "Psychic Research and the Resurrection," which was written twenty-five years ago by Dr. Hitchcock, who was then head of the American Society of Psychical Research, or if you were to read Sir Oliver Lodge's books, you will find that these men will say that very rarely could they definitely and positively affirm beyond any element of doubt a communication with a discarnate entity, who was consciously present and voluntarily delivering a message! It is too much a stretch of my imagination to believe that you or I, or anyone else, can call all of the spirits that we ever knew to us! Such an idea is perfectly ridiculous, in my estimation.

I knew Mrs. Curren, who wrote "Patience." One time I was in a group of people watching her. She sat at a desk, pounding the typewriter and smoking one cigarette after another, perfectly conscious and objective. She had very little formal education but was a very interesting person. She wrote a poem for each of us and the one she wrote for me was called "Jewels." It was done in the subconscious and was supposed to be dictated to her by a girl named Patience, who had lived in England about four hundred years ago. Some time later a group of people went over to England to investigate this claim and found that there actually was such a place where she said she had lived.

That reminds me of an incident told me not long ago. It seems that a girl has just recently learned to sing in three days an aria which usually takes about twelve years to master. Such is the power of Mind!

This incident is not without a moral. We may wait a hundred or a thousand years, or just a few hours or moments, I presume, to realize a truth that the illumined have discovered, or as has been said, "that which faith arrives at is already given." The gift of Heaven already is. Lowell said, "Bubbles we buy with a whole soul's tasking; 'Tis Heaven alone that is given away, 'Tis only God may be had for the asking." We may make many detours along the way. We may be so confused that we do not see the way. We may be so superstitious that we cannot find the way. All of us are more or less confused but we must not become more confused, but less. There is no such thing as the obsession of spirits. Sometimes it looks and appears as though there is, however.

A very interesting case of this kind that I had one time was with a woman who had a multiple of obsessions. I worked with her for three months before I could get her put together again. There were no spirits to get rid of, and finally one night I said to myself, "I am done with this nonsense. I know that these apparent entities are herself talking to herself. I know it, and this is the only Mind there is knowing what is true, and that is that." The next morning when I called on her, she said, "Last night these, whom I had thought were entities, came to me and said, 'we are not entities at all, we are only in your own mind.' " She was healed.

While working with her I had to get a line of thinking that would knock this belief out of my own mind, for it wasn't she who had to be healed, it was I who had to be healed. This is true with every practitioner whether he knows it or not, and with every case he takes, whether he accepts it or not. He may fool himself by saying the other person won't accept his treatment but that is working on the level of the psychic causation, which produced the confusion.

We do not depend upon hunches in our work and we must never permit ourselves to do so. I have no doubt that a complete and perfect psychic diagnosis can be made. If it came clear from the confusion, it would have to be accurate, but it has nothing to do with Spirit or with our work. These psychic disturbances are serious and we cannot say such cases are nothing and ignore them, for what is true on one plane is true on all.

There is the field of depth psychology, as it is called, where we remember when we were incarnated somewhere else. Personally, I do not believe in reincarnation. Other people may, if they wish to, but Dr. Rhine has proved that you can reproduce the activity of all the senses without using the organs of the senses, and now he claims in his latest book that you can think volitionally without using the brain. If this can be done, then there isn't anything on this plane of life that you would need to take along with you when you die! I maintain that we are as much Spirit now as we shall ever become.

It is much better to find that the mystery of the phenomena is in ourselves rather than in some alleged presence whom we haven't any reason to suppose is really present. It isn't logical, because all phenomena that are demonstrated including these alleged spirits, can be experienced with the knowledge that they are not real!

Though these psychic hallucinations are not real, the clairvoyant, clairaudient, and telekinetic powers which produce them are not illusions. However, they can produce delusions. The faculties themselves are faculties of Mind just as there are other faculties of Mind.

I am not confused about this field of psychism, and there is

113

no criticism in me about it, but it is a dangerous field for most people to work in merely because they let something control them, which I believe is in themselves no matter where it seems to be. We must accept the premise that psychic phenomena exist but we must interpret them in a dispassionate and sane manner.

The "revelations" of the ages are beautiful and interesting—Mohammed, our own prophets, and the Psalms. What is more beautiful than saying, "They that dwell in the secret place of the Most High shall abide under the shadow of the Almighty," or "The Lord is my shepherd, I shall not want"?

Have you heard the story about the man who met the Shepherd? An old minister and a young minister were attending a convention, and the young minister had just finished learning how to quote the Twenty-third Psalm very beautifully, and so he was asked to recite it to the assembly. He thought his recitation was good but there wasn't much comment made about it. He had everything it took as far as appearance and delivery were concerned. Toward the end of the day the old minister was asked to recite the Psalm too, and before he was finished everyone was in tears. Now the young man grew up to be a great minister because he went to another person present and said, "I know all the techniques of platform work; I have a good voice and I have personality plus, haven't I?" The other man agreed. "And wasn't my delivery of the Psalm dynamic; wasn't it good?" the young man asked. The other man agreed that it had been a beautiful rendition. "Do you think old Mr. so-and-so read it as well as I did?" "No," was the answer. "Well, then, what does he have that I haven't?" And the other fellow said, "Son, he has met the Shepherd and you haven't."

The man who said, "he that dwelleth in the secret place of

the Most High . . .," also said, in effect, "and God will put his heel on the neck of my enemy." That is pretty human stuff when we can get the heel of God on the neck of our enemy. We have him down and he will never get up again! We have always subjected our unsublimated, negative desires, whether it is the unconscious sense of guilt or some other disease, to God and asked Him to do for us what we couldn't do for ourselves!

There are just two kinds of religion in the world; one is prophetic and the other is ethnic. The prophetic religions are those which have come, apparently, into being through the special dispensation of providence and revelation. They are the missionary religions. When we read the revelations of the different founders of these religions, we find they all came from God. Do their revelations agree? No, for they are all psychic. They are automatic writings, really, and whatever the impulsion may be from the "other side" there is a great deal of confusion and interference. So we find in the psychic field, and in the field of alleged revelations, such a mass of contradiction that if we were to cancel out what each one, with apparent validity and certainly with sincerity, says the nature of God is, the other one says it isn't, and by the time we accepted them all we wouldn't have any God left! I say that the revelations of the ages are too contradictory and they are all psychic; they could not have come from the one source. God tells only one story—"I am that I am besides which there is none other."

This field of psychic hallucination, which has produced so much delusion, so much that is false and yet so much that is interesting, is a field that has to be handled very carefully indeed in order to find in it that which is true and real. I do not believe in spirit obsession. I do not believe in reincarnation because it answers no problems. It merely shoves the beginning of the time of a particular incarnation back a thousand or a million years in a timeless universe, to which a million years is as a day and a moment as eternity, and you have solved no problems. If reincarnation is true, we can't help it. We will have to endure it for there is nothing we can do about it. I have, personally, however, served notice on my universe that I am not coming this way again and there is nothing morbid in that. I just believe God has more in store for us, and that when we are finished here we will go on "there" into re-embodiment.

Let us turn now to the illumined people, to those few people—Dr. Bucke in his book "Cosmic Consciousness" cites fifty-eight authentically—who no doubt have brought to the world the greatest truths it has ever had and still does possess, and upon whose teachings Religious Science is based. As we turn to these illumined ones, we find there are no contradictions in what they have had to tell us; they all tell the same story.

First, suppose you and I send a body of people, whom we call psychics, one at a time beyond these mountains. We do not know what exists beyond them and so we send these people to find out for us. No one interferes with them and no one is there to talk to after they get there, or if there is, we do not know it. Then they come back, one at a time, and each records where he was, what he saw, and what he heard. After each one has gone and returned, we begin to compare their notes and find no two alike, and the contradictions in them are so inconsistent that they are impossible for us to accept. What would we say? We might examine these psychics and find that they are intelligent, sweet, and sincere people. Then each person must have seen what he says he saw, or

116

thinks he saw what he says he saw. However, because the stories are so dissimilar, there must have been hallucinations that were believed in, in complete sincerity.

If this could happen, then what is there today that I am believing isn't true? This means that we will have to discredit their evidence, for common sense refutes it. Logic and mathematics refute it. You cannot believe that something is and isn't at the same time! Yet, in these prophetic religions there have been certain mysticisms and always more good than evil. Even in our Christian religion we are better than we are bad, and that is all we can hope to be right now, in my estimation. We do not claim any ultimate perfection here in this world, and I sincerely believe there are plantings in this world which can bear fruit only in another one. Neither do I believe that the hell or the happiness that you and I experience, individually, is completely self-created. I do not happen to believe we are that good. You and I did not create the heavens and the earth, and "faith leads us to the place where *it* is given."

Remember the story of Job? This is a story with a moral, written by human beings, and it is a good one. Job was a good man. He fed his animals well. He took good care of his servants. He was a fine man and nobody knew it better than he did, but Job fell into a bit of trouble and circumstances went from bad to worse. Finally, Mrs. Job said, "Papa, there is nothing left so let us go out and die!" And Job said, "Well, Mamma, that is all right for you to do if you want to, but in spite of everything I know that there is an integrity in the universe, and in my flesh shall I see God."

The story goes on to relate that God "came down" and He and Job began to have a series of conversations and arguments. Plotinus, considered the king of the intellectual mystics of the ages, said, "If I were to personify God, I would say I do not argue, I contemplate." Here, however, was an argument and it was a good one. Job told God how good a man he was and God replied that He realized Job was a wonderful man. Finally Job works himself up into such a psychological superiority complex that it throws out the alleged inferiority complex, like a little boy whistling in the dark to keep up his courage, and he gets better and better. God listens to him and then says, "Job, you are a fine man. I didn't realize how good you are, but, Job, something has just come to my mind that perhaps you haven't been thinking about. I am pretty good too, Job. Job, where were you the morning I made the north wind and created the planets? I have been thinking and thinking, and I know you are a very good man, but I just don't remember seeing you around that morning? Where were you?" In the sudden realization of this truth Job falls on his face and exclaims, "You are right!"

In other words, faith takes us to the place beyond faith, to the acceptance of that which *is,* and this is what every great teacher who has ever lived has told us.

The realm of the spiritually illumined is the realm of the mystic, whether a Catholic mystic, or one living in the time of the medieval ages. The greatest of them all, I think, was Meister Eckhart. At any rate, they all tell the same story.

Now, let us send a party of these people over the mountain range to investigate what is beyond it. They have never been there and neither have we. Each independently goes and comes back with his story. When we put all the stories together, we find that except for the difference in language they all saw the same thing and heard the same thing. Wouldn't we say then that they had been to the same place?

Wouldn't we accept their evidence? This is the difference between the psychic and the mystic.

Mysticism is not psychism and it isn't mystery. Dr. Bucke defines it as "the direct perception of Truth." Intuition is the direct perception of Truth without any of the intellectual manipulations. However, it seems we must go through a process of reasoning to arrive at that which does not reason, but if it did reason, it would be reasonable. Jesus said, "I judge not and yet if I judge, my judgment is just."

It is to these mystics, to these spiritually illumined, that we must turn for such knowledge of the Kingdom of God as we may acquire to add to our experience of that which we all intuitively feel. Walt Whitman said, "There is more to a man than is contained between his head and his bootstraps." It pays us to read Eckhart, or St. Augustine's "City of God," or Saint Teresa. We should read Rufus Jones and Evelyn Underhill. It pays us to read Walt Whitman, Rudyard Kipling, Wordsworth, Whittier, and Robert Browning. Why? Because they are speaking the language, not of the unknowable, but of the unknown. They are the ones who bring news of the Kingdom of God to us and not the theologians, who have made up their minds that their God damns everybody who disagrees with them. There is no damnation other than our own little inner individualized "hells," which cool off as we gain confidence in the God that *is* and not the God that is often enough believed in. We find, too, that generally the mystic has come up out of some religious conviction or philosophic background, and as this cosmic, not psychic, experience comes to him he is redeemed from his own theology. To me this is very significant, for there is no mystic who ever lived who taught the concept of a hell or a devil. Eckhart,

119

who was a Catholic, was excommunicated from the church two hundred years after he died! It took the church that long to discover what he had been teaching.

Let us look to the illumined for the Truth. If anyone knew it, Jesus knew it. "Neither do I condemn thee; go, and sin no more," he said. He was projecting love but not deserting law. He knew that the two come together.

What have the great mystics taught? They have taught that every soul is on the pathway of an eternal evolution and all will get "there." Browning said, "I shall arrive as birds assume their trackless path." This, you and I will experience. These mystics have not even said this physical world is an illusion. Instead, they have said, with Plotinus, that everything is as real as it is supposed to be but nothing in itself in the objective world has self-determination. Spinoza said, "I don't say that mind is one thing and matter is another; I say they are the same thing." Jesus said that the Kingdom of Heaven is here *now* if we could see it. All of these men taught the processes of involution and evolution, and that the invisible is the visible. They have taught that love is the supreme good of life, and they have believed that all people are immortal now. They have all experienced the same "light." I have seen that light and it is quite a wonderful experience.

You might wonder why a person like myself had that experience, for you might say that I am not very evolved in consciousness. That has nothing to do with it. That is why the priests didn't like Jesus, for it was sacrilege to think that the sinners were in Heaven along with those who were saved! Most of us are so caught to negation that we would rather sing "My Rest a Stone" than to sing "God is all there is." We pray to God to save this miserable person that I am because we are too morbid to understand what Emerson meant when he said, "Prayer is the proclamation of a jubilant and a beholding soul." The world will some day drop all of this morbidity and psychism, because these mystics have come into the "light" in which they know there is no darkness.

> Whither shall I go from Thy Spirit, or whither shall I flee from Thy Presence? If I ascend up into heaven, thou art there; if I make my bed in hell, behold, thou art there.
> If I take the wings of the morning, and dwell in the uttermost parts of the sea; Even there shall thy hand lead me, and thy right hand shall hold me.
> If I say, Surely the darkness shall cover me; even the night shall be light about me . . .

> Yea, though I walk through the valley of the shadow of death, I will fear no evil, for thou art with me . . .

This is what the mystics have experienced but they have experienced it now and not bye and bye. "Beloved, now are we the sons of God." Anything that you and I hope of Heaven, they have experienced now.

I do not find one of these men being controlled by spirits or having a spirit guide. I do not find one of them preaching anything about reincarnation.

We can read anything into the Bible that we want to read out of it. It is unfortunate that most of the interpretation is read into it. We must remember that it was written by human beings and so use common sense in our reading of it.

Let us realize that if we know any Truth that someone else can tell us beyond what we directly perceive about God, and about human destiny, it will have had to come through these illumined people. I do not say this because I think they are elder brothers, or higher spirits, or high up in the hierarchies of life, for I do not believe in such concepts. I believe, however, that there are people beyond us in consciousness as we are beyond the tadpole, and we will come into that consciousness too.

In your practice and teaching never let yourself become disturbed or psychically confused. See if it doesn't make more sense to say, "I'm thinking what is happening, and what is happening by chance now can be reproduced at will." *Never* confuse psychic hallucination with Spiritual Mind Healing or the teaching of Religious Science. Do not let anything or anyone confuse you. Stay right with that dual Reality—the Law and the Word, the Presence and the Power, the Principle and the Person.

The practitioner does not depend upon hunches, or spirits, or phenomena. He depends only on what he feels within himself because he is keeping silent tryst with the Almighty God and with the Law of good. God, then, can speak directly to him. He lets no other candidate apply for room. He listens to that Divine Presence, unconfused and unconcerned in the many interesting things, mentally, subjectively, which rise out of the great collective unconscious. Out of it you can remember anything that is going to happen unless a new sequence of cause and effect, set in motion, changes it. Be harmless and wise, and above everything else, keep your heads. Do not let anything no matter how spectacular it may be suddenly bounce you off your mental feet. Our work is simple. It is direct. Let us keep it that way.

Your experience with Reality is all in your own mind, and here and here alone is your argument, your prayer. Your illumination or your hallucination shall ever be the act only of your own mind. The integrity of the universe has forever declared that the only God you will ever meet is within yourself! Let no one else interfere.

Come alone, sacred solitary, to face the great Reality.

Just as surely as we do the great Reality will respond. Only complete submission to It alone can solve our problems!

And so it is.

"The tumult and the shouting dies;
The Captains and the Kings depart;
Still stands Thine ancient sacrifice,
An humble and a contrite heart.
Lord, God of Hosts, be with us yet,
Lest we forget—lest we forget!

Far-called, our navies melt away;
On dune and headland sinks the fire:
Lo, all our pomp of yesterday
Is one with Nineveh and Tyre!
Judge of the Nations, spare us yet
Lest we forget—lest we forget!

If, drunk with sight of power, we loose
Wild tongues that have not Thee in awe,
Such boastings as the Gentiles use,
Or lesser breeds without the Law—
Lord, God of Hosts, be with us yet,
Lest we forget—lest we forget!"

From "Recessional" by Rudyard Kipling

EPILOGUE

The Sermon on the Rock

The three hundred or more people who attended the Religious Science Summer Seminar at Camp Sierra will never forget the very stirring message Dr. Holmes delivered before the assembly on the last evening of the conclave. No recording could be made of his talk but the words are indelibly written in the hearts of those who were present. On a mammoth rocky ledge in the high Sierra up above the little mountain village of Big Creek, where the group gathered to listen, Dr. Holmes stood with the majestic, pine-clad mountains as a backdrop and the slanting rays of the setting sun forming a canopy overhead. The hymn of praise and love and dedication which flowed from his heart was a fitting benediction to all who heard it. Small wonder that we were reminded of the Eternal Truths proclaimed in the "Sermon on the Mount."

Our leader and founder compared the strength we had received during the week to the strength and power generated in the nearby electric power plant, and, just as it served the valley below the mountains with its vast, stored-up power, did he charge us to go down into the valleys and carry the vision we had received and to impart the strength we had been given to others, to the end that our message of Truth and Love and Faith would spread to the whole wide world.

"Nothing of the eternal beauty of this week can ever be lost," he assured us. "Therefore, let us descend into the

125

valleys with singing and thanksgiving and let us henceforth live our lives so that, as Jesus said, 'Men may see our good works.'

"Religious Science is a practical philosophy of man's relationship to the universe and we believe it should always, and does, stand on its own feet. Ours is a simple faith. Like the rocks on which we are now standing it is unshakeable, permanent, and self-propelling; above the skyline of faith itself. Our belief rests on the divine idea that there is but One Mind, One Life—the Mind and Life of God. We are a part of that Life and Mind and all of us find our abiding place in our own consciousness. The God we are looking *for* we are looking *with* and *at,* and when we sing, we sing 'Love is the lodestone of life; lead on, kindly light, lead Thou me on!'

"We've had a dream up here this week, a divine dream of the spreading of our religious convictions and spiritual experiences, but dreams are not enough. We must act. We must demonstrate our spiritual rejuvenation and our unshakeable belief that Christ resides in all and that we are ONE. We must not only speak but act, and further than this, act with authority. Then and only then will the world accept and understand what we do.

"Let this be our motto as we go down into the valleys, towns and cities tomorrow, to put into action what we have experienced—*this I do in memory of this week!*"

"O, Thou Eternal God," prayed our leader, "we come to Thee with wide-open hearts and consecrated souls, ready to carry our message from You to all humanity, knowing now that we can and do behold the God in every man. Henceforth we do dedicate our lives to that which is true, to that which speaks of sweetness, to that which clasps us to Its bosom and which we, in turn, clasp to ours.

"Let us love one another; let us love the world. Let us serve simply and deeply, leaving the shouting and tumult to others. May the whispering of these majestic pines unify us with all creation! May the exquisite song of the birds and the caress of the summer breeze on our cheeks and the gentle warmth and radiance from the setting sun blend with the unspoken beauty in our own souls to make one divine and completely perfect creation, spiralling upward into the very vaults of Heaven, to rest there on the bosom of the Father forever.

"Thou, O Infinite Spirit, strip our egos naked bare so our naked hearts may find thy Presence there.

"Teach us, we pray, to love, and in Thy wisdom, make us wise. Amen."